To Ian Mc...
a fellow ...

L

Boy

Blue

Dave Farrell

David B Farrell

TRAFFORD

USA ▪ Canada ▪ UK ▪ Ireland

Note for Librarians: A cataloguing record for this book is available from Library and Archives Canada at www.collectionscanada.ca/amicus/index-e.html
ISBN 1-4120-8496-2

Printed in Victoria, BC, Canada. Printed on paper with minimum 30% recycled fibre. Trafford's print shop runs on "green energy" from solar, wind and other environmentally-friendly power sources.

Offices in Canada, USA, Ireland and UK

Book sales for North America and international:
Trafford Publishing, 6E–2333 Government St.,
Victoria, BC V8T 4P4 CANADA
phone 250 383 6864 (toll-free 1 888 232 4444)
fax 250 383 6804; email to orders@trafford.com
Book sales in Europe:
Trafford Publishing (UK) Limited, 9 Park End Street, 2nd Floor
Oxford, UK OX1 1HH UNITED KINGDOM
phone 44 (0)1865 722 113 (local rate 0845 230 9601)
facsimile 44 (0)1865 722 868; info.uk@trafford.com
Order online at:
trafford.com/06-0250

10 9 8 7 6 5 4 3 2

This book is dedicated to
"Old Desfordians" everywhere

and

In special remembrance of Dave (Pete)
and Shane who were called to that great
reform school in the sky, 2005.

I would like to thank my Wife Rosemary,
David Griffin, John Griffiths
and Ian Callaghan for their inspiration
and encouragement.

Further thanks are in order for my friends
Steve Middleton and Tony Redfern
for reading my manuscript
over and over again, and supplying me
with unbiased criticism.

I thank my daughter Emma for her tireless
efforts in producing a suitable cover.

My special thanks go out to Alec Jones
"A single ray of sunshine
during very dark days"

Contents

Foreword

I have no great axe to grind with the Social Services, The Home Office, Birmingham Children's Services or any other relevant authority for that matter. In fact, I bear no grudge or any ill feelings at all towards the Approved School and Remand Home Masters who administered beatings and corporal punishment to me with an exuberance that was far in excess of that which one would construe as acceptable punishment today. What's done is done! I have carried that Cross and worn that Tee Shirt for many years now.

I do not blame my mother. The poor soul must have spent much of her young life at her wits end just wondering where I was or what new shame I was in the process of inflicting upon her. For that Mom, I apologise to you with all my heart. I just hope that you can hear me and accept my most sincere apology, wherever you are!

I have no doubt that according to the laws and customs of the time that I thoroughly deserved the treatment that I received. One written report states that I actually liked being caned because I enjoyed the sensation. The mind boggles. That is not how I remember it at all!

I will not pretend for one second that I was a good little boy really, a veritable little angel whose mouth was incapable of melting butter, and that I was not responsible for my actions. I, and those who knew me in those days, know perfectly well that this was not the case, yet neither was I the little monster that certain people claimed me to be, well, not all of the time anyway!

I can also say with complete honesty that I was totally aware of what the consequences of my actions would lead to and of the punishments that would be meted out to me if and when my misdemeanours were discovered. I just didn't care in the end.

In my defence, not that I really need defending, I would point out that times were very hard for us all. Slum housing, no money, no father, precious little to look forward to and an environment where four letter words, regular beatings and a high level of exposure to criminals and fellow delinquents were the norm. All of these things helped to contribute in some way to my fall from grace. That is not an excuse. Just a fact!

I have changed all of the names of the characters and some of the timings in my book in order to protect the guilty as well as the innocent. It is not my intention to point the finger at any particular person, alive or dead, or even to take a well aimed swipe at the system. I just want to tell you my story!

Prologue

I suppose it all started to go wrong on one of those famously bitterly cold and wet February nights in 1959. Barely seven and a half years old with the weight of the world on my puny little shoulders, totally unprepared and completely oblivious to the trials and tribulations that were to become central to my forthcoming roller coaster ride through boyhood to adolescence. It would be exciting at times, exhilarating, sad, happy, painful, frightening, heartbreaking, and even harrowing, but I was a resilient little devil really and would soon learn to cope.

"The world is your oyster" my dad had told me many times, but my world, my oyster was inner city Birmingham. The district of Balsall Heath with all of its poverty and its crumbling cold damp terraced council houses forms the backdrop for my story.

The Social Services, through their seemingly endless list of psychiatrists, social workers and probation officer's reports had deemed me to be "A socially retarded emotionally disturbed delinquent of well above average intelligence!" Read on, and judge for yourself!

ONE

A Lesson in Humility

I knelt, half soaked by the drizzle beneath the warm glow of the cream and blue gaslight, cutting my initials into the lamp post with the pen knife that my dad had bought me for Christmas. "What are you doing David?" The loud gruff voice startled me, but I recognised it instantly. I glanced sideways, looking up to see the enormous bulk of Chalky White advancing towards me out of the darkness of the next entry. "Nothing Chalky" I shouted back feebly as I quickly scrambled to my feet.

He glowered at me from the edge of the shadows. His chubby round face had lost its customary smile, his lips tight now, almost snarling, as the lamplight cast its eerie yellow flickering glow on his furrowed brow, making him look very serious and even more menacing than usual. "Yes you are and its Mr White to you!" Oh shit, he looks mean! "You are vandalising my lamp post!" He shouted even louder as he thrust his enormous right hand in front of my face. My heart skipped a beat, or maybe twenty or thirty as I quickly realised he was not in the best of moods!

Just half an hour earlier I had been trudging wearily up my own entry, wringing wet, cold and shivering after skipping the afternoon from school to play in the old empty houses in Conybere Street that were earmarked for slum clearance. I had gotten carried away with no thought of what the time might be, but my rumbling stomach and the onset of tiredness had served to remind me that I did have a home to go to and a mother that would be worried sick about me. I began to creep the last thirty yards or so, mindful of the fact that at least one pair of nosy beady eyes lurked behind each set of curtains.

I reached the top of the entry and paused for a few seconds, motionless, holding my breath, listening intently as my eyes darted from side to side. Something was not right. I had a strange feeling that I was not alone. I could almost feel the blood rushing through my veins as my stomach churned. Slowly, I began to inch forward.

I knew it! As if by magic, my mother appeared from out of the shadows behind our makeshift fence, made up from the remnants of my father's pigeon pen. It was a well practised trick, more than worthy of any magician or illusionist. She seemed to have a sixth sense that told her when I was near.

"Is that you David?" She knew damn well it was. Her loud shrill voice and sudden appearance had startled me, stopping me dead in my tracks. Her eyes were blazing, brimming full of anger as she studied me, just waiting for a response. "Where have you bleeding well been then?" She had taken me by surprise and I could see that I had caught her on a bad day so I had to think quickly. The last thing that I wanted to do was incriminate myself.

"Out!" was my simple reply. "What's for tea?" I answered quickly and cheekily, for it was all I could think of at the time. I could tell that the wise thing to do would be to make sure that I remained well out of her reach, after all, I had been here before on more than one occasion and had a pretty good idea what was coming next.

"Never mind what's for bleeding tea! Where have you bleeding well been?" "I told you! Out! What's for tea?" Not a very good idea raising my voice to my mother! The long pause told me that I was trying her patience to its fullest extent. "Stew!" She shouted back at me with a tone in her voice that more than convinced me I was for it. Ah, well! I might as well get hung for a sheep than a lamb! "Stew!" I shouted back at her mockingly, making sure that everyone could hear me loud and clear. "Stew again ....just like last night and the night before that!"

The neighbours' doors began to open and curtains began to move in the windows of the Victorian terraced back to back houses that made up both sides of our entry. The door of the house to my left creaked quietly open as a non-descript neighbour took up her position on the step, leaning casually against the doorframe, the light from her living room highlighting my mothers face and showing me just how angry she really was. I was centre stage now and I knew it. A feeling of nervous excitement gripped me as I braced myself and prepared for the first battle of the day.

"That's right everybody, we are having stew to-night, just like we did last night and the night before that. In fact, I bet we have fucking stew tomorrow fucking night as well." Her face grimaced and her lips tightened, adding shame and embarrassment to her angry beauty as I screeched cockily, mocking her, swearing at her in front of the nosy neighbours. What the hell! I learned most of the swearwords from her anyway!

The woman to my left tittered as my mother began to advance, slowly at first, her body poised ready to pounce, her arms held high, just waiting for the right opportunity to grab me. She was almost in touching distance when she made her move.

"Come here you little bastard", but I was far too quick for her. I was off like a racing snake, back down the entry into Hick Street, leaping from the pavement as I gathered speed, straight past The Wellington Public House and on my way, back towards the freedom of the bomb sites and the derelict houses in Conybere Street.

I paused on the corner of Upper Highgate Street to take in the smell of the fish and chips that wafted through the open doorway of the local chip shop, and at the same time gave a cursory glance behind to see who was following. Nobody! Good! The rush of blood warmed me as I panted heavily, waiting patiently until I was sure that the coast was clear before slowly making my weary way back to the lamp post at the bottom of our entry, wondering how the hell I was going to get out of this one. The smell of the freshly cooked chips rested deep in my nostrils making me feel all the more hungry and wishing, not for the first time in my young life, that I had not opened my big mouth!

Chalky's big bulging eyes were staring down at me now as he stooped toward me, his enormous hand still in that menacing position right in front of my face, his breath reeking of stale beer and cigarettes. "Do you notice anything unusual about my hand David?" He spoke in loud menacing tones that had me wishing I was definitely someplace else. "No" I said with a whimper, "Mr White, I don't". This is not the Chalky that I know. This man is frightening me! I could feel a tear beginning to form and a dryness in my throat as he gruffly ordered me to look again, but this time, more closely.

I knew that he used to wrestle and box in the booths so it was not the prettiest of hands to have thrust in your face, and the smell of cigarettes coming off it was enough to make me feel like vomiting, but I managed to hold my constitution long enough to point out to him that he chewed his fingernails and his fingers were all yellowed and covered in Nicotine. "Is that all" he bellowed as his face began to turn purple, his big bulging eyeballs growing even more prominent and looking as if they were going to burst at any moment. By now it was quite obvious to me that I had given him the wrong answer. Please ground, swallow me up! "Look again", he snapped. "What do you see?" I looked again. "No, only nicotine" I said like a twat.

My head nearly disintegrated as he grabbed it with his crushing right hand and lifted me clear off the floor, straightening his huge body as he lifted my squirming scrawny frame in one quick, but obviously well practised movement. Cold fear consumed me as I wriggled, swinging my arms wildly and kicking out pathetically with both feet as I tried to shake myself free of his powerful grip, but the heel of his hand in my chin, his thumb and little finger in my cheeks and three fingers digging into the top of my skull made me quite powerless to break free. I could barely breathe and wanted to be sick for I could now taste the yellowness of his fingers, never mind smell it as he continued to crush my head with his iron grip. After what seemed like an eternity he growled at me "My hand is bigger than your fucking head and I don't like the way you talk to your mother!"

With that pearl of wisdom, he cast me to the ground like a rag doll, and, as I lay tearfully gasping for breath on the pavement beneath the gas light he just turned around and wandered nonchalantly back into the shadows, muttering in the cold wet night and leaving me to ponder the wisdom of my earlier actions. How I wished my Dad was here. I really missed him.

So, what shall I do now? I am most definitely not going home tonight! That decision, as it happened, was going to cost me a Juvenile Court appearance and three weeks locked up in Moseley Road Remand Home.

I know! The empty houses two entries up. I think

I will hide out in one of those for a while. As long as nobody sees me go in, I will be quite safe.

I could hear Jimmy Kelly getting yet another good belting off his eldest brother as I sneaked under their living room window and into the old house next door. His dad was dead, just like mine. Is that what happens when your dad dies? Everybody else just beats you up!

At least it was dry in here, though not very warm at all, but anything would be better than spending the night outside or going home to face the anger of my mother. Chalky had already taught me a lesson in that department, but she would not see it that way. She would want her own personal pound of flesh. I don't blame her for that because I knew deep down that I deserved it, but I just wasn't in the mood for another thumping. Not tonight anyway!

I crept up the dark narrow winding staircase, one step at a time, very carefully, very slowly and very quietly, barely breathing, trying desperately not to make them creak or offer out any sound, however slight, that might give me away. I made my way into the largest of the two bedrooms, stopping in the doorway for a full minute as I let my eyes adjust to the half light. The dusty old brown moquette armchair in the far corner of the room was a godsend, even though it was probably covered in fleas. The tatty old ripped and fire damaged blanket on the floor did not look so inviting, but it served as a good muffler when I placed it under the casters of the chair, enabling me to quietly drag it across the room to the open window.

I just sat there on my newly acquired throne gazing out into the cold wet night, wondering what to do next while I listened sadly to Jimmy's squeals through the walls as he continued to receive one almighty beating from his brother. I could almost feel the slaps as they rained down on him. Every now and again it would all go quiet, only to start up again with a ferocity that I could only imagine.

"You're always like this with the drink inside you!" Jimmy's mother screamed out as she pleaded for him to stop. I could hear it all from my ringside seat. Raised voices, shouting and swearing, his two younger brothers and his sister pleading with that bastard of a bullying elder brother to leave him alone, but as usual, it all fell on deaf ears. I can only assume that he finally stopped hitting him out of sheer exhaustion!

My eyes were getting quite used to the dark now so I had a good look around. I loved playing in the old houses, but I had to be quiet tonight. I certainly didn't want Jimmy's brother to hear me. The old houses had a definite smell about them. I never could quite put my finger on what it was, but it was a damp, musty smell that left a slight bitterness in the nostrils. I always thought that this was probably the smell of death that my grandmother often talked about after she had returned home from laying out some poor unfortunate soul.

Every bedroom had a scruffy little gas fire with coiled wire elements, set in a cast iron grate above an ornately tiled hearth. Tears in the brown stained wallpaper revealed painted walls of either yellow or green beneath it, obviously the council colours of the day. Great lumps of plaster hung from the ceilings revealing cracks and holes in the laths that had probably been there for a hundred years or more.

Every shelf, upstairs or down, seemed to be littered with old pills, dried up medicine bottles, safety pins and sewing needles, and there was usually a piece of wartime memorabilia on the linoleum covered floorboards, like a gasmask or a ration book. Every room had the remains of an old gas lamp, left over from the days before they were wired for electricity, and, they were all spooky! There was always an atmosphere that made me feel that I was never really alone, almost as if someone was standing behind me, an invisible presence constantly looking over my shoulder and scrutinizing my every move. Could it be my dad?

Was it true that god was always with us, no matter where we went? Could he really see and hear me every second of the day? Did he really know my every thought? Had he heard me swearing at my mother tonight? Well that's what Father Flynn said when he overheard me swearing in the playground. Or was it ghosts? Probably nothing more than my over active imagination running away with me!

TWO

Farrell v Flynn

My dad had died just a few weeks earlier, 31st January 1959 to be exact. He was only twenty six years old. "You are the man of the house now David!" My grandfather had quite proudly informed me of this while my dad's body lay on view in the dim light of our living room on the morning of the funeral. Grandad, that was my dad's dad, looked very important in his navy blue pinstriped suit as he rocked back and forth on the heels of his highly polished black brogues with his thumbs hooked under his braces as if they were holding his arms up. "Yes my lad, you're the man of the house now! You have to look after your mother and your brother and sister now son. Quite a responsibility for a lad so young as yourself, but you are a clever boy David and I know that you won't let me down". Let him down! That's a laugh. Oh well, at least he was half right. I was a clever boy alright, and that's a fact!

Having no father gave you definite advantages in life, free school dinners to name but one! We ate our school meals in a massive green Nissen hut alongside the school playground. I think it was a left over billet from when the troops were stationed here during the last war. It served as a Scout hut, Brownie hut and Guides hut in the evenings. It was also the school gymnasium by day and home to certain lessons in the afternoon such as the dreaded Folk dancing with Miss Brownley. More on my pathetic attempts at folk dancing later, for in a few months time I was going to be supremely enlightened. I was going to realise that I am definitely different to everyone else! In fact, for a short while I would believe that God actually listened to me, personally!

It all started with school dinners in the Nissen hut, and that most fearsome and most obnoxious of all Catholic priests, Father Flynn! He was a tall thin bony man with a face straight out of a horror comic. His skin was stretched tightly across his skull giving him the appearance of a living skeleton. His beady eyes sank well back into his head, which was rather shiny on top with a little black hair at the back and sides. A pair of gold rimmed spectacles perched proudly on his beak-like nose giving great depth to his icy stare. He always wore the same tight fitting black cassock with a high collar and a row of buttons straight down the front from the collar to the hem, just halfway up his shins. Shiny black leather boots with cross-over laces up to his knees made him look like an extremely ugly female Gestapo officer with a definite tendency towards sadism. I had seen the like many times before in the one shilling war comics that did the rounds at school. His voice was loud and nasal with a strong Irish accent. I hated listening to him ranting on from the pulpit and ruining all those lovely hymns with his tuneless nasal renditions at the top of his voice.

Father Flynn often kept an eye on us during school dinners. He would strut proudly between the tables with his hands clasped firmly behind his back, his head tilted back and his chin thrust forward, pursing his thin lips and casting his half closed eyes triumphantly about the room, glorying in the fact that he was quite obviously the master of all he surveyed. Very often he would have a tipped cigarette firmly gripped between his protruding yellowing smoke stained teeth, and, if you were ever unfortunate enough to be singled out by him while he was smoking, he ensured that you coughed and spluttered your way through his observations of your shortcomings and inadequacies as he blew great clouds of filthy grey smoke into your face.

Every now and again as the noise level of the chatter rose, he would clap his hands together and shout "Silence! Sit perfectly still". This was the cue to put your knife and fork open on the plate, arms straight down by your sides and prepare yourself for a mini-sermon while your chips or semolina got cold. It was during these silences that he would often question some poor unfortunate boy, usually me of course. This could be about anything from the Holy Trinity or the Stations of the Cross, to him having heard that I was cheeking one of the neighbours the night before.

"And what has Mr Farrell been up to today?" he would ask loudly in his own inimitable mocking nasal tones while the rest of the pupils looked on, barely trying to conceal their tittering. "Nothing sir" was my stock reply, to which he would come back with "Father to you boy, Father!" "Yes Father" I would meekly answer in a pitifully submissive voice as I silently said to myself "You ain't my fucking dad mate!"

"Quite the little gangster, aren't we Mr Farrell!" Where does he get this fuckin' we from? "You haven't been out of the remand home for five minutes, yet here you are sharing your dirty filthy little jokes with all and sundry!" The sly bastard must have been standing behind me! "No doubt you picked up these filthy little stories from your contempories in the little house Mr Farrell, or did a clever little chap such as you make them up all by himself?"

He grinned sarcastically, enjoying himself immensely as the rest of the pupils continued to titter and snigger, all of them quite obviously taking great delight from my current predicament. I looked down at my dinner in an attempt to hide the embarrassment that I could feel creeping slowly over my face. "Tell me one of your famous little stories Mr Farrell. I would just love to hear!" "Don't know any Father" I whispered quietly as I began to turn scarlet. "What was that you said boy? You don't know any!" "No Father!" "Look at me when I am talking to you boy! Look at me!"

His eyes pierced mine and I could not shake off the eye contact. "So, you are a liar as well young man!" He paused as his eyes sought a reaction from me. "Don't you know it's a mortal sin to tell lies to a priest?" he questioned as his long bony fingers slithered across the table and snaffled a handful of my chips. "When the last trumpet sounds young man, you will have to answer to God!" He continued to stare into my very soul as he slowly chewed on my chips, licking the grease from his thin bony fingers when he had finished. Bastard! "Carry on" he shouted triumphantly. "Mr Farrell and I will continue our conversation some other time."

I finished my meal and my dirty filthy little joke without further interruption from the screaming skull. Thank God another teacher had come to relieve him for his own dinner break. I hope he chokes on it after pinching my chips. Unfortunately, he did not, so there we were again going through the same routine the following week, and the week after that, and the week after that! The words would change slightly. One week I was a gangster, the next, no more than a pitiful little tearaway that deserved a damn good hiding, but the message was always the same.

It was a glorious sunny day in September, and our first day back at school after the summer break. I had enjoyed a good morning in my new class and had just eaten a more than welcome dinner in the Nissen hut. Father Flynn was on playground duties while I stood on the wall of the Boy's toilet with Stephen Phillips trying to catch a glimpse of the girls spending a penny next door.

"Come here you dirty little beasts!" His unmistakeably stinging nasal voice rang out across the playground. "Yes, you two, you filthy little creatures!

Come down here at once!" My pulse raced. I had taken a few cracks to the head off him before and it was not very pleasant. He had this knack of being able to catch you right on the eyebrow with his long bony fingers, and believe me, it bloody well hurt.

The whole playground had come to a grinding halt. Every child in the playground stood stock still, staring at us as Hula hoops slowed and clattered to the ground in mid flight, skipping ropes dropped, and footballs and tennis balls continued to roll down the slight incline towards us. The silence, broken only by the sudden sobbing of Stephen Phillips was almost terrifying. "My mom will bloody well kill me Felvy" Steve whimpered tearfully.

I had only two choices! Leap onto the spiked railings below and impale myself before the school, or climb down and meekly surrender to the vicious grinning bastard. I was still contemplating my fate when it happened. The miracle I had prayed for all these long months. "I said come here you disgusting little creatures!" He shouted with an uncharacteristic quiver as he pointed his accusing finger directly at me.

Then it happened! The answer to my prayers!

His voice began to fade away, echoing into the distance as he clutched at his chest with his left hand. He tottered unsteadily for a second or two, wide eyed, a look of shock replacing the grin on his skeletal face, his mouth wide open, gaping, and then suddenly silent as he gave one last searching look up to the heavens. His eyes flickered and rolled. His skin began to pale as he sighed heavily, letting out one last deep throaty gasp before his legs crumpled beneath him. For a few more seconds he remained bolt upright on his knees, his hands clasped together at chest height as if he was going to pray, then slowly, almost deliberately, his limp arms fell to his side and his body twitched before falling forward to the ground with a dull thud, quite dead.

Suddenly, I became acutely aware that the disbelieving awe filled eyes of the whole school were upon me.

The playground burst back into life with a deafening roar, everyone shouting and screaming. Two of the teachers came running across to the stricken priest and tried to revive him, fortunately, to no avail.

Steve and I had crept down off the wall by now and began to mingle with the other children, hoping that our part in this episode would pass by unnoticed, but we all know what hope did, don't we! The accusing fingers of the whole school led Mr Preece straight to me. Steve had disappeared into the encircling crowd!

The headmasters' retribution was swift and furious. My ear almost trebled in length as he dragged me kicking and squawking across the playground, through the side door and up the stairs to his office. As he administered the fourth stroke of his well used cane to my already bruised and battered backside his study door opened with a creak. "The ambulance is here sir; and a policeman" a teacher reverently informed him.

He looked at me, his eyes blazing, a twisted almost agonised expression on his face, almost as if he was horrified at the sight of this miserable snivelling little wretch weeping before him. "Get out of my sight" he screamed at me, "Get out! Now, before I do something I might regret!" I had never seen Mr Preece so angry before, so, not being one to ignore sound advice when it suited, I was off. Straight down the stairs, out into the street and away to the sanctuary of the old houses, wiping my tears and rubbing my sore backside as I ran.

Stephen Phillips was sat on a crumbling red brick wall, crying pathetically. He looked at me imploringly through his tearful blood-stained eyes as he wiped the tears from his cheeks with the back of his hand. "What am I going to do Felvy" he snivelled. "My mom will fucking well kill me!" He always called me Felvy. I am not sure why but the name just stuck. He always seemed to have a problem pronouncing his R's. Maybe that was why.

Steve's mom was a real old battleaxe, so I had a good idea as to why he was frightened. She was a great big fat piece with arms like Garth, a mouth like granny's sideboard and a vicious temper to boot. Her grey hair was always covered in a mass of tiny metal curlers, covered with a floral patterned silk headscarf which fitted like a turban. She always seemed to be wearing the same old flowered pinafore with the sleeves of her dress or cardigan rolled up above the elbow as if she was waiting for a fight. When she spoke, everyone listened, or cowered down in gentle submission like a puppy dog.

His dad was a tall thin frail man who, for all intents and purposes, had no opinions of his own and seemed to be completely grateful to his wife for allowing him to do her bidding, but at least he had a dad. I was envious of that.

I could not really understand why Steve was crying. He didn't give a monkeys' cuss about the sudden and unexpected demise of Father Flynn, and he was probably totally unaware that the headmaster had dragged me away for a dose of the cane and that he would probably be next. It was more than likely due to the sheer fear that he felt for his mother! She had told him on many occasions not to play with that David Farrell from Hick Street. "He was a thoroughly bad boy who will only get you into trouble. Mark my words!" she would say, "That lad is born to be hung!"

However, killing a priest was one thing. Defying his mother was infinitely more serious!

We strolled aimlessly around the bomb sites in the afternoon sun, picking and poking our way through the seemingly endless piles of junk that littered every pathway, entry and alley. We discussed our immediate future, mainly his actually because I had already had my caning, and decided that the best course of action was for Steve to run away from home. "You will come with me, won't you Felvy? I wouldn't know what to do on my own!" "Of course I will Steve. You're my best friend!" Another bad decision on my part that was going to cost me a further court appearance and another three weeks in Moseley Road remand home! What the hell. I've been there before!

THREE

A Night Out

My mind wandered back to that dark, cold and wet February night. Jimmy's screams had subsided some half an hour previously. All was quiet and it was very late. The single gas lamp in the entry had dimmed and I was feeling very sleepy. The rain had slowed to an occasional drizzle and the fresh wind carried the noise of the steam engines chuffing away in the nearby shunt yard to my ears. I had often lain awake at night listening to the engines through the open window of the small bedroom that I shared with my younger brother and sister, Michael and Bernadette.

Sometimes you could see the red glow of the hot coals lighting up the dark night sky as the firemen opened the boiler doors to shovel more coal in, and the sparks crackling and spitting, flying up in the air as the engines chugged and chuffed their way through the night. I would just lie there, listening to the clanking sounds of the chains and the bump of the engines as they picked up freight wagons bound for destinations far away. As the engines began their journey there would be an almighty judder accompanied by the squeal of steel on steel as the wheels raced, taking up the strain of the load.

I would lie on my back in my bed with my eyes tightly closed, arms straight down by my side, stretching my legs to make my body rigid and imagine myself sat cross-legged on the roof of the cab, arms folded with the wind and smoke in my face as I travelled the tracks to far off countries in search of adventure and untold riches. My dad was always the driver, dressed in his blue uniform complete with shiny brass buttons, grinning from ear to ear as he leaned out of the cab tooting the whistle with one hand and waving at the admiring onlookers with the other. My brother was always the stoker, smiling away as he worked feverishly, wringing wet with sweat, his bare arms and chest covered in coal dust, with a red and white spotted handkerchief tied tightly around his head like a gypsy or a pirate as he fed shovelful upon shovelful of coal through the open boiler door! No journey would be too long, no country too far, and no treasure too heavy for us to carry home. In my dreams, I had it all!

I felt comfortable and safe now. I began to doze. Where are you dad? When are you coming back home? I imagined him walking slowly up the entry towards me, a giant of a man with outstretched arms, beckoning, looking for me, always smiling and whispering my name as I drifted off to sleep.

I was awakened with a start by the sound of a dull thud! It sounded like a carefully planted footstep on a loose floorboard. A few seconds passed, then a creak, closely followed by faint scraping noises, almost like a series of squeaks. Something was moving! Very slowly and very carefully, but something was definitely moving. My heart began to beat hard in my chest. I could sense that it was quite close to me, but I could see nothing. I listened harder. It sounded more like something sliding now. Yes, definitely something sliding! I rose slowly and perched on the window ledge ready to drop onto the ground below and run. I could feel the fear building up inside me as the scraping sounds continued. I began to sweat profusely. My breath was shallow now, the adrenalin beginning to take hold. Slowly, noiselessly, I slid my right leg over the sill and, with my back to the window sash and my eyes firmly fixed on the darkness of the bedroom; I prepared myself for an extremely swift exit.

I saw a flash of movement out of the corner of my right eye. It was just outside the window! My heart leapt and my body froze. I dared not breathe lest I give myself away. The noise grew louder. I gripped hard on the sill, moving my head slowly as I forced myself to look in the direction of the movement. It was coming from Jimmy's house. I recoiled in horror as I saw the grey shape slowly emerging from the window next door. My heart raced as it slowly became clearer. I leaned out, stiffly, craning my neck for a better view.

The toothy grin of Jimmy was a more than welcome sight as he made his exit through the bedroom window, perching on the ledge as if ready to jump. I don't know who was more surprised, him or me. We both remained silent as I offered him my hand. He clasped my wrist tightly, looked me hard in the eyes and nodded urgently, obviously his signal to pull him carefully and quietly onto my window ledge and into my adopted but temporary home.

We whispered nervously together. What was I doing here? Why was he here? What shall we do now? We can't stay here! We pondered long and hard on our plight, looking for a sensible way out of the situation that we had become embroiled in. We talked at length about the death of our respective fathers and how we missed them so much in the short time since they had been taken away from us. We wept quietly together before slowly drifting off to sleep on the old armchair.

Just before the dawn we were awakened by the screaming of Jimmy's mom echoing from the bedroom next door. "He's gone, he's gone" she screamed over and over again. "It's all your fault, your fault, you drunken evil bastard". The screaming brought butterflies to my stomach. I could hear her throwing things, probably at Jimmy's brother as she screeched at the top of her voice. Her cries echoed across the yard, up the entry and through the open window of our haven. Jimmy cringed as we listened to her muffled footsteps clumping quickly down the bare wooden staircase. Within seconds she was out in the yard with a slam of the front door, shouting, screeching, "Jimmy, Jimmy, where's my little Jimmy" as she cavorted like a demon in her shabby green and brown tartan dressing gown.

Instinctively, we dived down onto the floor together to avoid being seen as one by one the neighbours came out of their terraced houses to see what all the commotion was about. We were so close that we could hear everything that was going on, but we dared not peer out for fear of discovery. "Are you alright Rosie?" a woman asked. "Whatever is the matter with you?" She continued to wail, though much quieter now as she managed to stutter out the fact that Jimmy was missing. Jimmy gripped my hand tightly, sniggering and making faces as he listened to his distraught mother.

"Calm down now Mrs Kelly, calm down" a deep, firm voice instructed her. "What's all this about then?" I recognised the voice of the local bobby. He had had occasion to lecture me several times since the death of my dad. How did he get here so quickly? My mind raced. Jimmy's mom continued to gasp for breath as once more she tried to explain the overnight disappearance of her son.

"Mrs Kelly! Does your lad happen to be a friend of young David Farrell by any chance?" the bobby enquired. "He's missing too you know!" We could barely conceal our excitement as our names were bandied about together. "I knew that cheeky little bugger would be involved somewhere along the line" squealed the tearful Mrs Kelly in her squeaky Southern Irish accent. "I knew there would be a good reason somewhere. That boy's trouble, mark my words! Nothing but trouble he is! I wouldn't mind betting that the little brat planned this and talked my Jimmy into going with him!"

You stupid venomous cow I thought silently to myself. What about that bullying twat of an elder brother. He couldn't possibly have anything to do with it, could he? Perish the thought that Jimmy might have run away because he was sick and tired of getting the living shit kicked out of him! Come to think of it, I haven't heard the big bully at all today. I bet he's hiding in the house. Gutless twat!

My name was mentioned several more times by the faceless voices that had gathered outside, nothing very flattering of course, but I was well used to that by now! We heard enough to know that the Police had been out looking for me all night and that the local bobby was on his way to my mother's house to tell her that there was no news of me. This obviously accounted for his rapid appearance in the entry.

"Right then! Listen in, all of you!" In his customary slow measured tones the bobby proceeded to address the small crowd that had gathered just beneath the window. "Young Farrell hasn't been seen since about nine of the clock last night and his poor widowed mother is worried sick about him. He appears to have run away from home for absolutely no reason at all. In my experience, young boys do not run off on their own, so I would lay a fair bet on the two of them being holed up together somewhere". Jimmy beamed and whispered his approval of him being linked with a lad of such ill repute as me. I'm famous, I thought quietly to myself.

"As I said" the bobby re-iterated, "His poor mother has absolutely no idea why young Farrell should do this." The lying cow! She knows exactly why I didn't come home last night, and while you are at it, why don't you try asking Chalky White the same question? I was beginning to feel angry now, almost on the verge of leaning out of the window and shouting the truth down to all of them, but I knew that would achieve absolutely nothing!

"And then there's young Jimmy! His mother also has no idea as to why he should do this thing!" What a lying bitch. Jimmy rolled his eyes and slowly shook his head as he looked at me, an expression of despair on his face. I felt truly sorry for him. Why doesn't she tell them about Jimmy getting the belting last night? Surely all these god fearing catholic neighbours must have heard something. Most of them could hear a ten bob note hit the floor half a mile away! "And, we have reason to believe that young Farrell is still in the area since the night patrols have not spotted him walking the streets!" Christ, I'll be for it now! I had no idea that anyone would go to all this trouble.

"Now, good people, you all know that the police force is extremely busy and we can do without the inconvenience of a couple of young tearaways playing silly buggers, so, I need a little help from you all". There was a short silence. I froze! "He is going to search this house" I whispered to Jimmy. "Don't worry Dave, they won't find us" he said flashing his toothy grin at me. "I have a hiding place in here! I've built my own den in the loft!"

The Bobby continued. "I want you all to get your warm clothes on before you catch your death out here, and then we will conduct a search of the old

31

houses, sheds and gardens in the immediate vicinity. I'm away to see Mrs Farrell now so let's meet back here in half an hour".

It was bitterly cold that Saturday morning. The wind had dropped during the night and the rain had subsided. It was fully light now and the winter sun was just beginning to shine through our window, lighting up the bedroom behind us. Jimmy and I had stayed warm by huddling together on the armchair, but we were both beginning to feel the cold now.

We lay perfectly still on the cold linoleum covering of the bedroom floor for a full five minutes as we listened to the muttering crowd slowly disperse. We were lying on our backs now, looking at the cracks in the ceiling and the exposed laths under the broken plaster where the rain had got in leaving long brown and yellow stains in its wake. Cobwebs were strung from the old glass light bowl which hung in the middle of the room. They looked quite pretty with the odd ray of sunshine highlighting the silver threads that seemed to peter out halfway across the ceiling. "What a dump!" I said to Jimmy. "It's a right shithole! No wonder no-one lives here anymore. It's almost as bad as our house!"

"He's a bad one, that Farrell kid" I heard a man's voice say. "Clever at school so I've been told, but rotten to the core. Always in trouble that lad". "His father was far too soft with him" a woman's voice piped up. As if! What does she know? "And you should hear his filthy language. Bloody disgusting so it is!" "Too right, but we all know who he gets that from, don't we!" "Indeed we do, and it wasn't his father, I can tell you!" "Father Flynn shamed him at mass last week, and the boy's not even a bloody catholic" another woman chipped in. I didn't know that! I really must go to his church more often! "I don't let my kids go near him" someone else interjected, but it really didn't bother me since I had heard it all before. Escape was my immediate concern now, so just hurry up and scuttle back into your two up one down back to back scruffy little terraced hutches and let me get on with it!

We stood well back in the bedroom, out of sight in the shadows, peering over the top of the window sill as we watched the last of Jimmy's neighbours disappear. We gave each other a cheeky wink as we heard the last door slam shut. We knew we were safe now, for the next half hour at least, as long as we kept quiet and didn't do anything to give ourselves away.

FOUR

Escape or Die

The loft access was located in the ceiling at the top of the stairs, right above the small square landing. The hatch had been removed and was leaning against the banister. The banister was lying on the floor of the other bedroom, having been previously pulled off the staircase wall. "That's my ladder over there" said Jimmy as he pointed to the broken banister. "I just hook it into the corner of the hatch and climb up. It's dead easy!" Sounds simple enough I thought to myself. Let's give it a go then.

"Okay then Jimmy, let's do it!" Carefully, and very quietly we lifted the banister and positioned it in the corner of the open hatch. Jimmy climbed up first, resting both feet on my shoulders as he groped around blindly in the loft for a hand-hold. He dragged himself up, turning quickly to sit on a rafter and offering me his hand for a pull-up. I gratefully accepted and within a few seconds we were both kneeling at the opening, peering down at the staircase below.

"This is my den" he said as he produced the stub of a candle and proceeded to light it with a match taken from the box he had concealed in the pocket of his jacket. "I hide up here all the time. Nobody else ever comes up here".

This was my first time in a loft. I had often seen the hatches as I played in the old houses in Conybere Street, but I had never been able to summon up the courage to enter one on my own. After all, anybody or anything could be hiding up there just waiting for a nosy little tearaway like me to pop my head up! Then what!

By the light of the flickering candle I could see that the loft was covered in a layer of thick black dust and that huge cobwebs were strung between the upper rafters. Yuck! That meant huge spiders. Chimney breasts rose out of the ceiling like castle keeps, all the way along in the middle of the roof space, one for each back to back pair of houses. Thin shafts of white light shone through the many small gaps in the slates, partially highlighting the collection of old boxes and various bits of junk that were casually strewn about the place. I was surprised to see that there were no dividing walls between the houses. This gave us the opportunity to crawl from one end of the block of houses to the other without fear of detection, as long as we remained quiet and trod carefully. "Don't forget to keep your feet on the rafters" Jimmy whispered "Or you'll fall through the bloody ceiling!"

This was definitely the best den I had ever seen! Why hadn't I ever thought of this? "Sometimes" Jimmy whispered quietly and slowly, "You can hear people talking in their bedrooms, making noises and doing things". My ears pricked up when he put a slight emphasis on "doing things". I paused, looking searchingly into his mischievous eyes. "What do you mean by that Jimmy, doing things?" I enquired with a sudden interest. There was a mysterious tone in his voice that held my attention and told me that I needed to know more. "You know" he said slowly, "Things! Things that men and women do together, when they are on their own, together!"

I thought quietly for a second, looking again at the impish expression on his candle lit face. "No Jimmy, I don't think I do know". I paused, looking into his eyes, wondering if he was telling the truth or just having me on. "What things do men and women do when they are on their own, together? What are you on about?" "Jesus! Don't you know anything?" He looked at me as if I were dense! "You know" he whispered, "Things! Like when my uncle Shamus comes over from the pub every Sunday afternoon. He gives us a tanner each to go out to Sunday school, and then he comes up here with my mother."

"What, up the loft?" "No you daft twat! Into her bedroom! He thinks we're bloody daft! I sit up here listening to them!" I hadn't a clue what he was talking about, but I felt that I most definitely needed to know more. "My brother says they call it shagging!" He began to explain to me in his own inimitable way and with great authority on this particular subject exactly what this shagging thing was all about. I felt a little embarrassed, and wondered how come he seemed to know so much about it while I knew nothing; after all, I'm supposed to be the one with all the brains!

I thought hard for moment, wondering again if he was taking the mickey or if I was just plain ignorant. "No Jimmy. They can't all do that. My mother wouldn't do anything like that", I informed him with a slightly raised voice. "Shushhhhhhh!" he whispered. "Somebody might hear us". "I still don't believe you" I told him in no uncertain terms. "Not everybody does it!" "They do I tell you, they do. I've seen them through that small crack in the ceiling by the light bulb!" I thought again for a second or two as I glanced towards the crack. "Well your mom might do that, but mine wouldn't" I told him with an air of superiority. "That's bloody disgusting!"

Before he could reply a voice rang out from outside. It was the local bobby, back already. "Right you good people, give me your complete and undivided attention please! Can I have the men on one side and the women and children on the other, please?" We heard the crowd muttering as they shuffled around and into position. "That's good" he said, "Very good. Now, ladies, I want you take your kids with you and search all of the gardens and outbuildings in the immediate vicinity. Pay particular attention to garden sheds, coal bunkers and the outside toilets. You men! I want you to search the old houses from top to bottom. You two can start with these houses here, the rest of you follow me over to Conybere Street". He paused for a few seconds. "Well, go on then. Get on with it! Away with you all now!"

The noise level rose as the crowd outside went about their allotted tasks. Coal bunker lids crashed and banged as they were lifted up and dropped again. We took the opportunity to creep down to the bottom end of the loft under the cover of the outside noise where we found an old pair of dusty curtains. A thick piece of dusty wood leaning against the wall at the end of the loft came in handy for us as a make-shift perch. We set it down on the rafters behind the last chimney, lay on it together, blew out the candle and covered ourselves with the curtains. We were just in time!

We listened with bated breath as we heard the two men clambering into the living room through the open window. The front door was secured with a large metal padlock. "Anybody in here?" a strong voice shouted. Neither of us recognised it. "You don't expect 'em to fucking well answer do you?" the other voice mocked. Terror-struck, we realised that the second man was Jimmy's eldest brother. "Christ! Of all the people it could have been it had to be him!" groaned Jimmy. "He'll fucking well kill us both if he sees us!"

"Well, what have we got here then?" Jimmy's brother shouted as he noisily climbed the stairs. "A fucking banister propped up into the loft! I bet the little bastards are up there!" We began to panic. "What are we going to do?" We asked each other. "He might not see us" Jimmy said hopefully. "It's fucking dark up here". "Pass me the fucking torch" his brother rasped "I'm going up there!"

We listened carefully as he climbed noisily into the loft, not daring to move a muscle between us. I could feel the waves of panic beginning to consume me as I heard the other man pass up the torch and start the climb to join Jimmy's brother. I peeped through a small hole in the curtain and could see the yellowy beam of the torch flitting against the wall behind our chimney as Jimmy's brother flashed it up and down the loft.

"Can't see anything" he mumbled to himself. "Jesus, they must be up here! That banister was too much of a fucking coincidence so it was, and I'm almost certain I can smell candles!" He said in his rich Irish brogue. "I bet they are hiding behind one of those fucking chimneys, so they are! Come, on. Let's have a fucking look. You can stay by the hatch" he ordered the other man, "Just in case they try to escape through it while I'm up the other fucking end!"

He started for the other end first. "Come on Jimmy, come on out. Your mother is worried to fucking death about you!" he shouted. "Come on Jimmy, I know you're fucking well up here, and you know I'll find you in the end! I won't hurt you Jimmy, honest I won't!" "Not fucking much" whispered Jimmy with a tremble in his voice. "He'll fucking well kill us both!"

I suppose it only took a minute or two to reach the other end and get back to the hatch although it seemed like an eternity to us. We huddled there, stock still and in complete silence behind our chimney, not knowing what to do next. Last night wasn't the first time I had known him give Jimmy a real belting. I had seen it before so I knew exactly what the bastard was capable of. I wondered if he would fare so well against Chalky White. The answer to that question would be revealed much sooner than I would have anticipated! "Fucking bastard" Jimmy whimpered. "I hate him! I wish he would fall through the fucking ceiling and die!" Suddenly, it all became very clear to me. I knew exactly what must be done!

"Nothing up that fucking end" Jimmy's brother said loudly to his mate. "They must be up here some-where!" With that he began to slowly advance towards us, carefully picking up his feet, treading softly as he shone the torch downwards to ensure that he trod on the rafters. I could feel the ceiling moving as he picked his way from rafter to rafter, slowly but surely edging closer towards us. "Fucking cobwebs" he said. "I'm covered in the fucking things". My heart was in my mouth, beating twenty to the dozen. I began to shake with fear as he continued to make his way to-wards us. Blind panic gripped me as he stood a yard from the curtain that covered our huddled bodies. "What the fucks this then?" he shouted menacingly. "You're not under the fucking curtain now, are you Jimmy?"

With a blood curdling shriek I leapt up, straight at him. He shouted out in frightened surprise as I threw my puny body against his and caught him full in the chest, knocking him clean over with the sheer force of it, and sending him crashing down through the ceil-ing and onto the top step of the stairs below. Luckily, I managed to grab hold of a roof beam, hanging on tightly to prevent myself from falling with him.

It all happened in a flash. I looked down at his motionless body lying at the top of the stairs covered in lumps of plaster and broken lath. Great clouds of plaster dust swirled around him. I was sure I had killed him. "Come on Jimmy, come on. Let's get out of here!" I shouted as the other man started to scream out at us. I dropped down onto the stairs next to Jimmy's brother. Jimmy was with me in an instant. We almost fell as we raced headlong down the stairs, around the corner at the bottom of the staircase, past the coal-hole under the stairs and into the living room. It was empty. I opened the front door and we fled out into the blinding daylight.

"There they are" the woman from next door shouted at the top of her voice. Too fucking late you old bag! We were off! A leap over the small garden wall into the entry, a left into Hick Street and another left towards Belgrave Road in the opposite direction to Conybere Street saw us well on our way to freedom. I glanced up my own entry as we hurtled past. People shouted at us in the street to stop. No fucking chance of that!

The excitement almost overwhelmed me as we bounded across Belgrave road leaving all in our wake, up the first entry, out through the other end past the Alms houses, a right over the wall into another entry and out into Sherbourne Road. We ran like the wind through the back streets and alleys of Balsall Heath until we could run no more, eventually coming to rest in the sanctuary of the trees in Cannon Hill Park.

We sat there in the thickest part of the wood, breathless, red faced and beaming at each other. I laughed out loud when I noticed how filthy we were, covered in the thick black dust and cobwebs from the loft. Our hands and faces were black and I noticed a large tear in the sleeve of my jacket. Fuck it! It just didn't matter anymore.

Jimmy broke the silence. "I think you killed my fucking brother I do!" He paused. "Will they hang you?" "Dunno Jim" I replied as the seriousness of my actions began to dawn on me. "Well I never liked him anyway" he said. "The bastard was always giving me a good hiding. It's been like that since my fucking dad fell off that scaffolding". He began to cry softly into his hands. I put my arm around his shoulder to comfort him.

His dad had died just before Christmas 1957. I remembered all the talk of the accident. He was a scaffolder on the new block of flats that were being built in Leopold Street, just around the corner. Jimmy was six at the time.

My own dad had fallen victim to Myeloid Leukaemia. I watched him wither from a giant of a man who neither smoked nor drank into a shuffling skeleton. Neither of us understood death. We just heard about it. My fathers' funeral was still fresh in my mind since it had taken place only a few weeks' previously, but Jimmy could remember very little about the fate of his father, just that he fell off a scaffold and would not be coming home anymore.

It was still quite early, about ten in the morning

and we were feeling very cold, hungry and thirsty. I knew we could not stay here so we got up, walked around the woods for a while and decided to find something to eat. First stop was the public toilet in the park for a drink of water and a clean up. Next, a visit to the hothouses in the hope of pinching a couple of bananas from the tree that was set by the goldfish pool, provided of course that the attendant was not around. No such luck!

I knew that it would be no good trying to nick the pennies that people regularly threw into the goldfish pool as they made their stupid wishes. I had tried that one before and almost got caught. Besides, it was quite deep.

We wandered around the hothouses and gasped in fake amazement at the wide variety of plants on show. We split up for a while, hoping that the attendant would follow one of us, leaving the other to snatch the bananas, but he never budged, and he never took his beady eyes off us for one second. He just sat there underneath the banana tree, staring at us as if he knew exactly what we were up to. Oh well. At least it was warm in here. I must have spoken too soon! "Come on then lads, let's be having you" the attendant shouted to us. "We close at twelve, open again at two!" "Okay mister" I said politely. "We're going now".

The double doors slammed tightly shut behind us. I heard the key enter the lock, turn and click loudly as the tumblers of the lock fell heavily into place. It was a sound I was going to find all too familiar over the next few years of my young life! What now I thought, what do we do next?

We hung around the woods in the park until the darkness began to close in, spending most of the afternoon climbing trees for a bit of fun and building a den out of broken branches and Laurel leaves so that we had somewhere to sleep tonight. We talked a lot about the events of the last day or so, whether or not it hurt when they hung you, were we ever going to find something to eat and if we really thought his brother was dead. We spoke of our fathers, wondering what they would think of all this if they were still alive, then listened quietly as the park keeper went around chaining the wooden gates shut. The last gate to close was always the enormous wrought iron double gate which secured the road adjoining the hothouse, leading out to Edgbaston Road and alongside the cricket ground.

We looked on as the keeper drove his blue City of Birmingham Parks Department Morris Minor van out of the final gate, parked up on the road outside and proceeded to wrap the thick metal chain around the upright railings. He completed the operation by securing the chain with a heavy duty padlock before climbing back into his van and driving off into the night. We were on our own now.

FIVE

Welcome to Desford

I lay warm and snug between the Home Office issue brilliant white cotton sheets, staring at the moths flitting to and fro around the yellow night light. The familiar smell of the starch on the stiff cotton pillow cases, although pleasant, served only to remind me that yet again, I was a long way from home. I was not overly bothered about the black eye for I had received several over the past few years. My aching ribs were no cause for concern either, but despite the relative safety of a warm bed, I felt decidedly threatened, and although surrounded by twenty four more boys of a similar disposition to myself, once again, I felt quite alone. It was April, 1963. This was the first night of my first day at Desford Boys Approved School.

It had been a long tiring day. Along with a dozen or so other boys I had been noisily awakened for a six o clock breakfast at Kingswood Classifying School near Bristol. We had been locked in there for three long miserable weeks of tests and assessments, and this was our big day. The powers that be had finally decided which particular Approved School most suited our particular talents for disruption and petty crime.

My stay at Kingswood had not been a happy one by any stretch of the imagination, due mainly to the fact that I was one of the smallest and youngest of the boys being held there. This had led to certain advances from some of the older boys, and bullying when refusing to perform some of their frequently requested personal favours. Fortunately however, I had already learnt how to cope with this situation in Moseley Road Remand Home, so it came as no great surprise to me. In fact, I had expected it! And, although I had picked up many bruises along the way, my virtue remained intact!

Within the hour I was showered, clothed, fed, booked out and aboard the navy blue Police mini-bus clutching a small brown suitcase that contained all of my worldly possessions. I found myself gleefully looking back at the twelve foot wire mesh perimeter fence as we drove out through the open gateway and sped down the long straight drive. Despite not knowing where I was going, and the knowledge that I was likely to be spending the next three years there, I was glad to put that dog hole behind me!

Our first stop was an approved school near Portsmouth. We were only there for a few minutes. Three names were loudly and clearly called out by a burly policeman. Three boys got off. A man wearing a grey jacket and trilby waved his walking stick as he ordered the three to stand to attention next to a large red brick ivy covered wall. He eyed them up and down carefully before signing three sheets of paper for the policeman. He climbed back aboard the bus, job done, and we were back on our journey. Thank god for that, I thought silently to myself. I didn't fancy that place one bit!

It was a strange subdued atmosphere on board the bus. We were not allowed to speak to one another but the policeman sat at the rear of the bus broke the silence every now and again as he pointed out the different landmarks, towns and villages along the way. His commentary droned on until we eventually arrived at a group of large cream and green coloured Nissen huts behind a tall wire fence, apparently in the middle of nowhere. The place just seemed to spring up!

I managed to find out that we were somewhere in the Cotswolds. "Out you get" a policeman said in a loud rasping voice. We all filed out and stood in line with our cases while he called the roll. "Answer Sir, when you are spoken to lads". "Yes sir" we answered as one, having already been well drilled in the art of replying to our superiors.

A cheerful looking master appeared on the sun-lit courtyard where the minibus had been parked. A group of older boys dressed in blue overalls walked behind him in a line, each one carrying a garden hoe. They were all smiling, jabbering away to each other in excitement as they came to greet the new boys. Oh well, I thought to myself. This is more like it! It doesn't look too bad here. At least everybody looks happy. As the policeman called the roll each boy answered in turn and was ordered to step forward. The master eyed each boy up and down before signing the sheet and directing them toward the older boys. Every boy that is, except me.

"Come on young Farrell" the policeman said. "Let's get you fed and watered. I dutifully followed the three policemen across the courtyard, alongside the well trimmed grass verge and through a green wooden door in the side of the largest hut to reveal a spacious dining room. Young boys, all dressed in grey pullovers, short grey trousers and grey socks were casually drifting in through the open double door at the far end of the hut and forming a line near the hotplates. They seemed happy enough as they chatted amongst themselves whilst running a suspicious eye over me. I was ushered towards the hotplate at the front of the queue and handed a tray. "Get on with it Farrell. You must know the routine by now" one of the policemen said rather disdainfully.

I picked up a soup dish and held it out in front of the server. "Hello Dave" a voice piped up. It was my cousin, Lawrence! He was a small lad who could hardly stretch over the hotplate to serve. My spirits lifted at the sight of a friendly face. "What are you doing here Loll?" I enquired excitedly. "Keep quiet Farrell! Just get on with it" a voice barked from behind. "Our Dennis is here you know!" Lawrence whispered out of the corner of his mouth as he poured a full scoop of Brown Windsor soup into my dish. "So are Jimmy Kelly and Gary Tucker!" Those were a couple of names that I had not heard for a long time. I had often wondered what had happened to them!

"Come on Farrell, move along" the voice behind

me barked, "And no talking!" I quickly collected my next plate and gratefully received my meat and two veg before selecting a cold rice pudding on the way to a remote table around the corner and out of sight of the rest of the boys.

I ate in silence with the three policemen as I craned my neck in an attempt to spot Dennis, Jimmy and Gary. No such luck! The memory of Lawrence behind the hotplate in his little white cotton pinafore apron complete with soup stains would remain with me for a long time, for it would be more than five years before we met again.

"Excuse me sir" I said almost pleading with one of the policemen. "Where am I going?" We were back on the bus now and Lawrence was but a memory. "All in good time young Farrell, all in good time" he replied patronisingly. I had long gotten used to being on my own but I was now starting to worry. Why would no-one tell me anything? I felt like a prisoner of war on my way to be shot in a deserted clearing, or maybe I was going to a special prison where I would spend the rest of my life in solitary confinement. Christ's sake! I wasn't that bad. I knew plenty of young lads whose behaviour was far worse than mine, I think!

We seemed to be driving forever. I sat quietly, clutching my suitcase on my lap, looking out of the windows as we drove through a changing landscape of long rolling hills separated by clumps of trees and small woods, arable farmland and fields full of sheep dancing away in the spring sunshine. It was a far cry from my roots in inner city Birmingham. As we drove further north the sky began to cloud over and darken. Small droplets of rain spattered the windows and made patterns on the glass as the rush of air generated by the speed of the bus forced them to the rear of the vehicle.

We pulled up at a roadside café where the driver got out and bought four china mugs of piping hot tea between us before re-claiming his seat at the wheel. I could tell from his demeanour that he was in charge. The other two had taken seats either side of me at the back of the bus, quite obviously to make sure that I did not attempt to run away.

For the first time they spoke to me in an almost friendly fashion as we sat in the bus drinking our tea together, listening to the pitter patter of the rain on the roof. "Not much further now son" said the driver in a warm and friendly voice. I noticed the three gold coloured sergeant's stripes on his arm for the first time. He sipped his tea as he stared at me. "Desford!" He paused. "Desford Boys School! That's where you're going to son. About eight miles the other side of Leicester. We should be there by three o clock". "Thank you sir" I politely replied. He returned the mugs to the café and we drove on.

"How have you found yourself in this mess son?" asked the policeman to my right. "Dunno sir." That was my standard reply when questioned by anyone in authority. "It just happened." Buggered if I'm telling them what a little shit I've been. They've only just started to be nice to me. Much to my relief they did not pursue that line of questioning. Instead, they began tell me what a lovely place Desford Boys School was and how I would be very, very happy there. In fact, they painted such a rosy picture of the place that it gave me the distinct impression they were taking the piss.

By now it was raining heavily. The windscreen wipers were working overtime, the windows in the rear of the bus were steaming up and the heating was full on. I dozed off to sleep without much prompting.

"Come on lad, wake up" one of the policemen said as he gently shook me by the shoulder. "We are almost there". I quickly gathered my senses and peered out of the window. It had stopped raining now. In fact it was so dry that it looked as if there had been no rain here at all. We sped up the long tree lined lane, took a right at Botcheston Jot and continued half a mile or so before taking a right into the long steep winding drive that was the entrance to my new home.

I could see the large ivy covered tower, its pointed roof and bright orange tiles dominating the skyline as we approached the crest of the hill where the school buildings loomed before me. A left turn took us along the frontage until we ground gently to a halt outside the two large heavy wooden doors that secured the front entrance to the school.

Compared to others that I had seen that day it was a daunting and most formidable sight. The mood of the policemen changed rapidly. I was duly ordered off the bus and told to stand at the foot of the steps with my belongings while the sergeant rang the bell.

After an agonising wait the door opened and I was led into the entrance hall where I stood holding my breath with my back to the wall while the policemen completed my formal handover into the charge of the headmaster, Mr Vernon Rees, before going back about their business without so much as a backward glance.

He was a tall stocky Welshman with a voice that instilled fear into your very soul, yet it also had a certain warmth about it. As I was destined to find out in the coming years he was a very hard man, but also, very fair and not entirely devoid of compassion. His very short back and side's haircut with a fingered compressed wave of dark brown brylcreemed hair petered out to his sparse greying sideboards. He looked very smart in his brown checked suit with a tie to match and highly polished brown shoes.

His piercing eyes were almost menacing and I could see that he was strong from the thickness of his arms and the size of his hands. I felt a little fearful, in fact, quite small and worthless as I stood before him. I could sense that he was weighing me up in his own mind, wondering just how much of a problem I would turn out to be. I braced myself, waiting for him to start the ritual ranting and raving that I had become so accustomed to while he informed me what a worthless individual I was. This never happened. Much to my surprise, he sat me down at a chair in his board room, had a ten minute friendly chat, laid down the usual rules then took me to the linen room to collect my kit.

All of my new clothes had a white tag stitched into them bearing my new number embossed in bright yellow cotton. "A1! That's your number Farrell, A1!" he said. "Will you be A1 Farrell? It's a hard number to live up to! Can you do it Farrell?" he inquired. "Dunno sir" I replied as I slipped back into defensive mode, realising that his friendly banter had put me off my guard. "Dunno!" he said threateningly. "Oh, I think you will young man, I most certainly think you will! It's not often we get a former grammar school boy in here Farrell, so I expect great things of you!" He paused before emphasising the point. "Great things!"

He carried on to inform me that in addition to the current houses of Fernie, Belvoir and Quorn, a new house was being formed called Atherstone. I was now Atherstone One, hence my new number, A1. He explained in great detail that all of the houses were named after local hunts and that Atherstone would not function fully as a house until the arrival of the new housemaster in about three months time, after the summer home leave. Meanwhile, until the house was fully up and running, I would be attached to Quorn and would take on the temporary number of Q42 for all house activities. These activities would include a variety of team games and sports for which we would receive house points, and that the house collecting the most points at the end of each term would receive one extra day's home leave per boy. House points could also be gained for good behaviour and individual achievement both in school and on the sports field; however, they could also be lost!

After the evening meal, I was placed in the care of one of the older boys who was directed to show me the ropes as it were, give me a short tour of the school, show me my bedspace in dormitory three then direct me to the medical room where I could be examined by the school nurse, Miss Franks.

I was feeling quite pleased with myself as I left the medical room at the top of the G.O. (General Office) corridor. No nits, no nothing. I had been treated very well and I had eaten like a king that day. I felt very comfortable and very smart in my light blue Terylene Vee necked sweater, and my grey corduroy shorts complete with striped elasticated snake belt. The long thick grey socks up to my knees were quite warm and even the black leather lace-up shoes had a bit of style about them and fitted perfectly. The rough grey cotton shirt was of standard issue, though I cared little for the oversized underpants that slipped down from my waist with the long legs touching my knees as I ran, but that was a small thing to put up with. I just knew I was going to enjoy it here as I started off in search of new friends.

I had probably taken no more than two steps out of the corridor when I bumped into the steamers! They were waiting for me, three of them, older boys with an unnatural yen for my arse, just by the entrance to the toilets. An arm flew around my neck and started to drag me into the toilet block while a pair of hands attempted to drag my shorts downwards. This was a situation I had encountered several times before at both Moseley Road remand home and Kingswood Classifying School. I did not succumb on those occasions and had no intention of doing so now!

I lashed out frantically with both feet and arms, kicking and scratching as I screamed out at the top of my voice for help. Nobody came! I twisted my body violently and tried to squirm free of their clutches. I took a hard fist in the right eye, but managed to grab the arm and sink my teeth deep into the fleshy part of my attackers' wrist, drawing blood as I bit deeply. Despite his screams and his struggle to free his arm I bit even harder, determined that he should not get away lightly. More blows rained down on my upper body, but, though only eleven years of age I was fit, strong, fighting mad and turning decidedly nasty, determined that my assailants would not get the better of me!

I shook free of the neck hold and lashed out again with my feet, almost burying my shoe in a steamers stomach. He fell back, winded. I swung out again with my fists at the steamer who had originally grabbed my neck and hit him square on the nose as he was about to retreat. His nose crumpled and the blood flowed out over his face and my clenched fist. I had the upper hand now and I was beginning to enjoy it! He had no more stomach for the fight and was off like a frightened jackrabbit, closely followed by his two accomplices. Although quite small for my age I was very strong in comparison to my peers, and the last few years of being regularly bullied, humiliated and ridiculed had given me one hell of a vicious temper!

I stood tall, red faced and almost breathless from my exertions, looking into the sea of faces that had gathered in the top corner of the playground to spectate. I could see no friends there! With a contemptuous look I turned about and walked proudly into the toilet block to clean up, hiding my true feelings as I winced with the pain and trembled with rage.

Hiding my true feelings was a necessary skill that I had painfully acquired over the last few years. I had learned very quickly that my feelings were a weapon that could and would be used against me to devastating effect if I allowed it, a weapon that I had found to be far more painful to me than a boot, a fist, the back of a hand, or even a cane!

There had been no master on duty in the playground at the time, either by design or otherwise. I knew I had to be careful from now on. I stayed quite a while in the toilet block, splashing cold water on my face to cool me down, washing the blood from my hands and waiting to see if there was to be a second attempt by the steamers, or indeed anyone else who just fancied a pop at me. None came.

A loud bell sounded from the direction of the playground. I guessed that this was some sort of command to do something. I walked proudly, erect, out into the cool night air, my face still burning and red with anger and saw the boys lining up by the outside entrance to the dining room corridor at the bottom left hand corner of the playground. I joined the line and followed them into the dining room. I caught the steamers gaze as they looked on while I stood proudly and defiantly by the centre pillar, waiting for a master to tell me where I could sit. I noticed that the seat I had used for my evening meal was vacant. The three steamers were sat at the adjoining table. I looked straight at them, and with a swagger, I walked over to take my place. I could feel the tension as I sat in silence and feasted again, this time on bread and dripping, washed down with a mug of hot, thick, dark brown cocoa.

The headmaster said very little of note in his nightly report. He asked me to stand as he introduced me to the school as the new boy. Fortunately, I was too far away for even his eagle eyes to notice the swelling that was beginning to surface and blacken around my right eye. We all sat and listened intently as he informed us all that the two boys who had absconded yesterday were in police custody and, due to the late hour would be returned to the school in the morning. On that note we were dismissed for vespers before retiring to our respective dormitories at a quarter to nine. Lights out was at nine o clock after which time there was strictly no talking and we were forbidden to set foot out of our beds, for any reason!

As I listened to the footsteps of the duty master fade away down the staircase and along the stone flagged corridor the whole dormitory, as one, broke out into a series of whispered giggles and chatter. Twenty minutes later all was silent, save the sound of gentle breathing and the odd snore of contented sleep. I lay awake a little while longer, still staring at the nightlight, thinking about the events of the day and wondering what tomorrow would bring before quietly crying myself to sleep. I found myself drifting back to that cold February night in 1959. I was seven and a half years old again!

SIX

A Stroll in the Dark

Jimmy and I were walking now, alongside the railway lines at the top of Moseley Road. We had slipped through a hole in the park fence and picked our way through the backstreets, carefully avoiding Edward Road police station and climbing the wall to the tracks behind the old Imperial cinema. It was a cold dry almost cloudless night with a slight wind. The crescent moon was high in the night sky, bright enough to aid our vision without silhouetting our bodies, so we trod quickly along the top of the embankment to keep warm, kicking the gravel as we went. We gazed up at the many stars that flickered and shone in the black sky. "I wonder which one is my dad" Jimmy said wistfully.

We were on our way to Hawley's Bakery, about a twenty minute walk away. I had scrounged many a cake or sticky bun in the past, usually when I was on my way to the ABC minor's Saturday morning matinee at the Alhambra. We could have chosen a quicker route, but this one suited our purpose well since the bakery was only around the corner from where we both lived. This route provided us with the cover that we needed, and besides, it was far more exciting!

We enjoyed it immensely as great black steam engines thundered past, belching smoke and sparks from the funnel and with great spurts of white scorching steam shooting sideways from the hoses behind the wheels, hissing loudly as it forced its way out under great pressure. We whooped with excitement and joy as we leapt down the embankment at the very last moment to avoid getting burnt by the steam or seen by the driver or the guard. We were close to Montpelier street halt, so the driver would give two short pulls and one long pull on his steam whistle as he hooted his warning signal. It was a sound I loved.

We carried on, past the rear of the remand home and behind the Friends' Institute, pausing at the bridge alongside the bakery and peeping over the top to see what opportunities would present themselves to us. We watched with great interest as the numerous trucks pulled in and out of the well lit loading bays whilst the workers pushed seemingly endless trolleyloads of cakes and bread onto the concrete platforms behind the trucks.

The night air was rich and full with the unmistakeable smell of freshly baked food. Our mouths watered profusely as we climbed down from our lofty perch, scampered across the road below and took up a position in the shadows on the near side of the bays. We waited for a moment or two until the coast was clear. I crept forward toward the concrete platform at the rear of the last truck while Jimmy kept watch for the driver. Still managing to stay in the shadow beneath the bright orange glow of the Sodium lights,

I carefully edged my way onto the platform and behind a trolley. It was full of ring doughnuts packed tightly into wooden trays that slid into runners on the upright trolleys like the drawers of a tall sideboard. Using both hands at once, I grabbed four doughnuts and quickly climbed back down off the platform. I hissed at Jimmy on the other side of the truck to follow me to the bridge. We climbed back up, sat together behind the wall and feasted on our ill gotten gains.

We were cock a hoop now, and brimming with confidence. We had food in our bellies, but we were still hungry. We waited for a few more minutes before we again took up our positions in the shadows. Once more, Jimmy crawled under the truck and took up his position behind the large wheel on the passenger side. He hissed the all clear, so I advanced slowly, albeit with a little less caution than I had previously displayed and peered over the platform. I could hear voices but could see no one. I listened carefully, hardly daring to breathe as the voices grew louder. Suddenly, the hard thick black rubber double doors from the bakery swung open, crashing against the wall with a resounding bang as more trolleys were pushed onto the platform.

I held my breath as two men talked while they stood less than a foot from my head, then listened intently as they collected a couple of empty trolleys and made their way back through the doors, their footsteps, their voices and the squeaking grinding wheels of the trolley echoing into the distance. Quickly now,

I leapt onto the platform once more. The coast was clear. I had a much better choice now. The doughnuts were still there, minus the four I had stolen just a few minutes earlier, but a few feet beyond them lay a better prize. One trolley load of freshly baked steaming hot bread, but, beyond that and much nearer to the rubber doors was a trolley full of assorted fresh cream cakes, just waiting to be devoured by my friend Jimmy and myself.

To this day I have never come to understand why I hesitated; after all, the choice was obvious. I approached the cakes, grabbing a warm loaf on the way. I glanced down the side of the truck at Jimmy's face peering out from behind the wheel, orange in the glow of the lights, and raised the loaf high in my left hand as I gave a triumphant grin. I was so full of myself that I had not noticed the expression on his face changing to a look of sheer terror as I placed the loaf on the floor and began to wrestle the whole top tray of cakes free from the trolley.

As I slid the tray free, still smirking triumphantly with my new found bravado, a huge hand cuffed me around my right ear, knocking me to the ground, the tray of cream cakes flying everywhere. "You thieving little bastard!" an extremely large burly man in white overalls shrieked at me. "You thieving little swine!" My head was reeling and my ear throbbing as I leapt up with tears in my eyes screaming at him. "Don't hit me mister, please don't hit me again mister. I'm hungry!" This was a ploy I had used with great effect on more than one occasion, however, this time it became quite clear to me that my pleas were falling on deaf ears as he swung at me again, knocking me hard against the bread trolley and sending me sprawling on to the hard concrete platform.

This man had obviously never heard of the word mercy and possessed not one shred of compassion. Excited voices rang out and the sound of running footsteps echoed across the platform. I looked up, dizzy and still reeling from the last blow. People were coming from everywhere to see what the fuss was all about. Still stunned, I staggered to my feet and leapt off the platform, dodging the swinging arm of the burly man as I went, and ran past the trucks, past Jimmy and into the road as the angry bakery workers gave chase.

"Come on Jimmy. Run!" I shouted at the top of my voice. "Run you idiot!" Too late! As I glanced behind at the two young men giving chase, I could see Jimmy being held against the front of the truck. He was caught, however, I was not, and I intended for it to remain that way. I hurtled onto the Moseley road as the two men continued to press me, pausing only briefly to check that no traffic was coming as I sprinted across the road and into Leopold Street. I glanced back again. They were still coming! I carried on down Leopold Street, took a left into Upper Highgate Street and down the hill heading for the sanctuary of the old houses at the rear of Conybere Street. I was breathless, gasping for air. I glanced behind again. Still, they continued to give chase.

I could not go to the old houses now. The piles

of rubble would only slow me down and I would be caught for sure. I turned left at Conybere Street heading back towards Moseley road. On the right was a factory, its side entrance protected by a small wooden gate, chained shut. I clambered over the gate and ran up the narrow entrance drive as fast as my legs would carry me, staggering, and then collapsing breathlessly behind a pile of wet cardboard boxes adjacent to the dustbins. I lay there not daring to move, my heart pounding, my stomach turning and my pulse racing, gasping quietly for air, listening hard as the rhythmic sound of their footsteps grew louder, then faded slowly as the two men ran past the entrance without so much as a second look, on their way back towards the Moseley road. Pair of twats! They were easily fooled!

I waited for a few minutes until I had gotten my breath back fully. I listened carefully, craning my neck to catch any sound that would betray them, just in case they had quietly doubled back to surprise me. When I was sure that the coast was clear I managed to summon up enough courage to creep back down the drive and peer over the gate. They were there, standing on the corner of Moseley Road, outside the Sir Charles Napier public house, looking up and down the street. They had a good vantage point, right on the corner of the crossroads. There was no way out for me here without being seen. I looked around in the moonlight and noticed a drainpipe leading up to a low flat roof with a small wall running along its length.

I climbed the drainpipe quickly and easily, pulling myself over the wall with both hands, crouching low as I looked around. I was certain that no-one had either seen or heard me! There was a small door at the far end of the roof and it was overlooked by the first floor windows of the factory itself. I tried the door. Locked! I tried the windows. They too were locked; however, one of them was broken and blocked with a small square of plywood, stuck flimsily on to the inside of the metal window frame with cellotape.

It took less than a minute to remove the plywood, put my arm through the window to release the catch, open it and climb inside. As I looked around in the half light I could see a desk positioned against a wall next to a pair of swing doors. A light on the staircase shone through the two circular glass windows that were set in the doors, giving me just enough light to see where I was going. I moved forward and examined the desk. It had one single drawer. I tried the drawer. It was open. Inside the drawer neatly laid out were various items of stationary, including a black plastic fountain pen. I slipped the pen into the inside pocket of my jacket. Another bad decision!

I shook with fear as I listened to the shrill bells of the approaching police cars, ringing out into the night as they sped towards the factory. I could not tell how many there were, but it sounded like the whole of the city police force had come to get me! Car doors opened then slammed shut as the policemen got out, shouting as they flashed their torches against the windows of the factory.

"Come on, we know you're in there! We've got dogs!" I almost wet myself at the thought of a large Alsatian tearing me to shreds. I kept quiet as the torches continued to flash against the windows, lighting up the ceilings and racks as they flashed along the whole length of the building. My mind raced, trying to think of a way out. I sat on the floor underneath the desk, out of sight, trembling with fear, wondering what to do next, too scared to move.

My heart leapt and my stomach churned so much that I felt sick when I heard the front doors of the building burst open. They were in! I could hear the loud footsteps as they raced up the stairs, dogs barking, and men shouting as they burst through the swing doors only a few feet from where I sat. The bright beam of a torch flashed straight into my face, almost as if they knew exactly where I would be. "There he is! We've got him!" I motioned to get up and run but they were onto me in an instant. A huge hand grabbed the collar of my jacket as I tried to crawl and bolt from the cover of the desk, lifting me onto the tips of my toes. I was blinded by the light of another torch as a policeman flashed it full into my face to inspect his capture. He paused, sighing as he stared at me. "David bloody Farrell" he said with more than just a hint of annoyance in his voice. "I might have known it would be you! It's a good job these dogs are on a bloody lead! Come on son. You've led us a right merry dance!"

SEVEN

Someone Must Pay

I sat on the scruffy old wooden bench in the holding room at Edward Road police station, reading the names that had been carved into it over the years. Nobody there that I knew!

Jimmy was already there when I arrived, but he had been taken into another room with his mother. A large policeman stood in the doorway, swinging a large bunch of keys on a chain, staring silently at me as if he had never seen the like before. I gazed around the room at the dirty white ceiling, the light green painted plaster walls and the huge, thick green metal door, open against the wall. I heard a woman's voice sobbing from the direction of the corridor. Unmistakeable! That's my mom. No doubt whatsoever about that!

She came into the room accompanied by a detective who allowed her to throw her arms around me, give me a quick cuddle and tell me how worried she had been before we were directed to an interview room. Her mood changed as I related my version of events to the detective. Wagging the afternoon off school, the stew incident, Chalky Whites lesson in humility, Jimmy's belting and the murder of his brother.

The day in the park, the walk along the railway lines, theft of a few stinking cakes and my ultimate capture in the factory! Mom was absolutely livid, though I could see that she was glad that I was safe. I didn't say so at the time, but deep down I was glad that I had been caught and relieved that it was all over.

Luckily for me, or unluckily, depending upon how you look at it, Jimmy's brother was alive and well. A bit bruised, a bit battered and somewhat stunned at the time, but worst of all, his huge ego had taken an almighty dent, and for that, someone must pay. No prizes for guessing who!

After signing the statements, I was allowed home in the care of my mother with a warning that criminal charges may be preferred against me. A swift crack around the head from mom and a mouthful of abuse from both of us as I ran past the babysitter on my way upstairs to bed was my lot for the night. I was glad to be back home and happy that I had gotten off so lightly, though I must confess that I had no idea at the time what the repercussions for that days work would lead to!

Mom bought me a bowl of hot stew upstairs with a chunk of crusty bread. She had calmed down now. I wolfed it down, burning my mouth on the thick dumplings as usual. My brother Michael was the next to appear in his nightgown, and joined me in the bed that we had shared for the past few years. Meanwhile, in my absence, our younger sister Bernardette had been elevated to the comparative luxury of a cot mattress on the floor of mom's bedroom. Mike and I chuckled and giggled together as I told him what had happened. Slowly, we drifted off to sleep.

Mom was quite a forgiving sort really. I got out of bed early on the Sunday morning and laid the fire exactly as my dad had taught me. That was my job and I was good at it. Mom made a pot of tea and a large saucepan full of porridge oats. That was her job, and she was good at that too! We ate our breakfast and drank our tea together as usual, just as if nothing had happened. The only difference being dad wasn't here with us anymore. We talked about him for a little while.

We laughed and cried together as we reminisced about the time that I swapped my brand new two guinea black and green herringbone overcoat with the rag and bone man for a goldfish and a plastic windmill, and the leathering that I got off my mom while my dad chased up the road after him to get it back! I apologised with all my heart for all the trouble that I had caused and promised faithfully that I would be a model son from now on and would never ever get into any more trouble. I would grow up and be the man of the house, just like my granddad told me at the funeral. I really did mean it at the time, honest, I did!

I strolled down the entry as our neighbours looked on in disgust. I smirked at them, as only I could, changing my walk to a cocky strut and staring them full in the face as I passed them by, saving a special sticking out of the tongue for Mrs Barratt as she slung her head back and rolled her eyes at me in

71

disgust. Fat miserable old bag! I was on my way to see how Jimmy had fared. He would be back from mass now. Another mistake!

As I turned to the right at the bottom of the entry, full of the joys of spring and not a care in the world Jimmy's brother pounced on me grabbing me by the hair, shaking me violently and slapping me about the face as he swore at me at the top of his voice. "I'll fucking well kill you, you little bastard" he screamed. I was petrified for I knew that he meant it. He threw me hard against the wall, punching me in the stomach as I bounced back towards him. I couldn't breathe. I staggered forward trying to get my breath, retching as he laid into me. Another punch, this time to the chest, then swiftly followed by an enormous fist to the head. I fell to the pavement, doubled up in agony, trying to protect myself from his boots. My heart seemed to stop for a few seconds and I could not even force myself to breathe. Everything seemed to be happening in slow motion and I thought I was going to die, right there and then. Suddenly, out of the doorway of the Wellington pub a great familiar voice rang out. "Oi, you! Fucking well leave him alone!"

For all his great bulk, Chalky could move like a pouncing Tiger. In an instant he had crossed the street, crashing his great fist into the face of Jimmy's brother, forcing him to stagger backwards. He suddenly looked dazed and confused. "How do you like it you fucking great bully?" Chalky hit him again, and again with no reply, clubbing him half to death against the wall as I looked on, prostrate, still gasping for breath on the pavement. "Not so fucking easy with someone your own size is it!"

It took several large men to pacify him, hanging on to his powerful arms as he struggled and cursed at the top of his voice, trying desperately to continue his brutal assault on my assailant. "Stop it Chalky, stop it! You'll fucking kill him! The bastards not worth it" they shouted. Chalky stepped back, visibly shaking with rage. His great purple face and bulging eyes were still brimming with anger as he eyed Jimmy's hapless brother lying on the floor, covered in blood and weeping pitifully. He didn't look so hard now!

A large crowd had appeared from inside the Wellington Pub. People flocked from the adjoining streets and entries, just like they always did when something like this happened. Chalky walked over to me and gently picked me up, cradling me in his arms as he asked me if I was alright. This was the Chalky that I knew! I could see that he was beginning to calm down now. He turned his head, looking hard at Jimmy's brother. He was lying on his back now, a well beaten man with a look of utter humility on his face as he forced himself to return Chalky's glare, knowing that he had more than met his match. "Get up you bullying bastard!" Chalky hissed at Jimmy's brother. "Get up and get out of here before I change my fucking mind!" He rose slowly and unaided from the floor, looking at me through half closed eyes, saying nothing as he turned his back and began to stagger away. I almost felt sorry for him. "Go on you bloody coward! Fuck off!"

Less than a month later I made my first appearance in the Juvenile Court. Steelhouse Lane in the centre of Birmingham was where it all happened in those days, right next door to the main police station. I stood next to Jimmy in the dock as a rather pompous sounding official who had positioned himself in front of the bench read out the list of charges that were being brought against me. We were in good spirits, confident that in a few hours time we would both be back home, laughing about it.

Theft, Burglary, Trespassing and common assault! I nearly fainted. Several policemen and a bakery worker gave evidence against me. A policeman reading from his notebook made me sound like a regular little Jack the Ripper as he described the way I leapt at Jimmy's brother like a demon possessed, knocking him through the ceiling and onto the floor below. I was flabbergasted! How could he possibly know that? He wasn't even there! He was the local bobby who had organised the search for us. My form teacher spoke on my behalf. I felt confident that I would be going home and very proud when she told them what a bright boy I was. Then she ruined it all completely by admitting that I was fast becoming a truant of some notoriety and at times disruptive in class with my constant chatter and cheeky remarks.

The Lady magistrate looked over the top of her pince-nez disapprovingly as she asked me to answer for myself. For a few seconds I was speechless. Quite a change for me! My mind raced as I wondered what I could say in my favour. I looked imploringly at her and her two colleagues at the bench as they exchanged knowing glances. I looked at my mother for inspiration. Nothing! Just her sad eyes, looking at me as if she already knew what the outcome of all this would be. "I'm waiting David!" Her voice was louder now, echoing around the silent courtroom. "What have you got to say for yourself?" I began to redden as the butterflies stirred in the pit of my stomach. "I'm still waiting David!" I had a very bad feeling about this.

"It's all lies your honour" I blurted out tearfully. "All lies! It wasn't like that at all!" She looked hard into my eyes, silently studying me for a few seconds. "David" she said in a soft, almost sympathetic tone, "Did you, or did you not push Mr Kelly through a ceiling and onto the floor below causing him to sustain injuries that required hospital treatment?" "Well yes ma'am, I did, but I had to. I thought he was going to kill me and Jimmy". She gave me a curious, almost incredulous look. I could tell that she did not believe me.

"And did you David" she continued dispassionately, almost in monotones as she read from her notes "Walk along the railway lines, illegally enter the premises of Hawley's bakery and steal several items of confectionary?" "Well yes ma'am, I did, but we were very hungry!" I tried to sound pitiful but I could see that she was having none of it! She exchanged glances with her colleagues once more. They all seemed to look at me as one, the same disbelieving look on each of their faces.

"And after that David, did you then break into the

premises of RJ Williams & Son, stealing a fountain pen from a desk drawer?" I took in a deep breath as I prepared to answer. "Yes ma'am, I did, but two men were chasing me. I was frightened and went in there to hide". She paused for a few seconds. I could almost see her mind ticking over as she stared silently at me, carefully considering my answers. She looked at her colleagues again, exchanging whispers, nodding and shaking their heads as all three perused the various notes scattered about the bench.

She looked hard into my eyes again as if searching for her own answers. "Tell me David" she asked deliberately, "In what way did the theft of the fountain pen help you to hide from these men?" Once more, I was speechless, positively dumbstruck in fact! My mind raced as she continued to look hard into my eyes, waiting for my answer. "It was only a fountain pen ma'am" I feebly replied.

Jimmy's charges were read out. Trespassing! That's it! I asked myself. Fucking trespassing! "How do you answer?" the magistrate asked politely. "Oh, I'm guilty alright" smiled Jimmy. "I definitely did that your honour!"

We sat silently on the long wooden padded seat in the dock while the magistrate whispered, nodded and shook her head in quiet, guarded conversation with her two colleagues at the bench. I picked away nonchalantly at the green leather upholstery, tightly held in place by a row of brass studs. My mind wandered as I stared out into space. The magistrates shuffled papers, made a few a notes, and, every now and then glanced in my direction. I could tell that they were not looking at Jimmy. After a few minutes, Jimmy was asked to stand up. He was given twelve months probation and excused from the dock. I watched with envy as his mother rose from her seat, a look of smugness on her face, and Jimmy, with his toothless grin as he avoided eye contact with me, met her in the aisle, clasping her outstretched hand as they left the court together, with an usher.

"David Bernard Farrell" her voice rang out again. "Please stand." I had a gut feeling that this was not going to be my day! "After careful deliberation with my colleagues, we have decided to commit you to a remand home for a period of not less than three weeks in duration, but not more that one month." I trembled as I heard my mother begin to sob uncontrollably. An usher led her from the court. "You will appear back at this court in three weeks time, by which time we will have considered their report. Take him away officer!"

The police sergeant led me from the courtroom through a heavy oak panelled door behind the dock, along a narrow dark corridor and into a small barren room containing just a table and two wooden chairs. He motioned for me sit down; saying nothing as he casually glanced out through the doorway. I listened carefully at the unmistakeable clickety click of high heeled shoes on the tiled floor, growing louder as they echoed down the corridor toward me, coming to an abrupt halt outside the open doorway. After a few seconds my mother appeared at the door, still sobbing, but not so heavily now.

We talked in the company of the sergeant for a few minutes. Another policeman provided us with a cup of insipid yellow, sweet tea. Neither of us had a chance to finish it. "David Farrell" a voice boomed out from the doorway. My heart leapt and I trembled as I tried to control the butterflies in my stomach and not let on that I was on the verge of wetting myself. "This way lad!"

Mom cried as I was led out into the courtyard and into the dark foreboding belly of the awaiting Black Maria. I glanced behind as I stumbled up the two metal steps to the waiting guards. I could hear my mother, still sobbing, but I could not see her anymore. I sat, trembling, holding back the tears as the doors slammed shut. I listened intently at the metal gates opening outside as I stared into the dark unsympathetic eyes of the guard opposite me. I lurched sideways as the vehicle accelerated through the gateway, turning hard left on its way to Moseley road remand home. Another chapter in my short life was about to begin!

EIGHT

A Rude Awakening

I was woken up with a start by the sounds of shouting and loud banging on the locker nearest to the entrance of dormitory three. "Come on you boys, wakey wakey, rise and shine. Come on! Out, now! Out, out, out!" I gathered my senses as I quickly leapt out of bed in obedience to the loud commands. This was the beginning of my second day at Desford Boys School and it was off to a flyer! I glanced quickly and nervously around the dorm. Boys were leaping everywhere, frightened looks on their faces as a tall thin lanky man in a grey suit bellowed out his orders at the top of his voice. He moved quickly amongst the boys, tipping the mattresses of those who were too slow to rise, still shouting loudly as they crumpled in a heap on the floor with their bedding, scampering and crawling as they fell. "Come on!" he shouted. "Up, up, up! All of you get up, now!" he screamed as his long legs carried him around the room at almost breakneck speed.

I followed the other boys lead and dressed as quickly as I could, hoping against hope that I would not be singled out by this fearsome, raging, noisy, devil of a man. When he was satisfied that every boy was out of bed he bounded out through the doorway, his thin face reddening with the efforts of his voice, his coal black eyes bulging and his head leading the way in earnest as his thin skeletal body followed down a few steps and into another dormitory, while we all listened as he repeated his obviously well practised wake up call.

Once more, I followed the lead of the other boys as they quickly made their beds, ready for his inspection. He bounded back up the stairs to us. "Any tankers?" he shouted sarcastically, and two boys who had folded their blankets and made their beds army style, sheepishly ran over to him clutching their wringing wet sheets. He shouted at them mockingly as he placed a mark against their names on the sheet attached to his clipboard, then motioned at them with the back of his hand as they scurried out of the dorm and down the stairs, still clutching the wet sheets that they had paraded before him.

He strode around the room with an air of supreme confidence and great authority as he inspected each individual bedspace in turn, again checking each name off before falling each boy out with an approving tap on the head with his pen when he was satisfied with their efforts. He paused to speak as he strode up to me. "New boy, eh!" he said. "Farrell isn't it!" "Yes sir" I replied as I braced myself for an angry tirade, not letting him see that he frightened the living daylights out of me. "Where did you get that eye?" He rasped. "I fell over in Kingswood yesterday sir". My pre-planned explanation appeared to work as he gave me a long suspicious glare, drawing his breath through his teeth and his tightly closed lips as he inwardly digested my excuse, asking himself if I was telling the truth. His face changed. He paused, my pulse quickened. "Well done" he smiled, "keep it up" before tapping me on the head and allowing me to follow the rest of the boys.

I scurried down the steps, glad to get away, following everybody else into the playground. The whole school was busying itself for early morning work details. I looked around, not knowing what to do as boys disappeared into the sett room in the top right hand corner of the playground, and then reappearing a few moments later clutching their cleaning utensils. Some carried a mop and bucket, some a broom, dustpan and brush while others clanked about with a scrubbing brush, a bucket and a brightly coloured rubber kneeling pad. They all seemed to know exactly what they were doing and where they were going. I was lost. I had no idea what I should be doing.

An older boy called out to me as I began to worry, realising that I stuck out like a sore thumb in the middle of the playground. The last thing I wanted to do was to draw attention to myself. I had already made up my mind to go with the flow, change my ways, do my time and get out of here as quickly as possible. Although I had been sentenced to three years I knew that good behaviour could see me freed on early licence in just twelve months time. This was my goal.

I looked across the playground at him. He carried a mop and bucket, a broom and a dustpan and brush. I thought it quite a lot for one boy to carry. His friendly face beamed out at me as he called me over, and I noticed he was different to most of the other boys in that he wore long trousers. "Come on" he said, still smiling "Lets get weaving!" He offered me the mop and bucket and we strode together to the toilets at the top of the G.O. corridor. "It's not bad here" he informed me, "once you settle in."

As we swept and mopped the toilets out he went on to explain to me that he was a house councillor in Quorn, hence the long trousers. Apparently, they were a perk of the job! "I'm attached to Quorn for the next three months" I said excitedly, hoping that the common ground would help a friendship to develop. "I know" he said. "Brynn Williams, the housemaster told me you were coming and asked me to keep an eye on you. He's O.K. when you get to know him. You will see him at the house meeting tonight. Just don't get on the wrong side of him and you'll be fine!" That sounded ominous. I'll have to watch it!

He carried on, and gave me a brief outline of the daily routine as we waited for the duty master to inspect our work. I felt much better now, not so lonely! I could get to like it here, I thought to myself. It's amazing what a difference a friendly face can make!

We continued to chatter about anything and everything in the toilet doorway as we waited, both of us confident that this was the cleanest that the toilet block had ever been. The tall lanky master who had woken me with such a start that morning had a quick look around before sending us off to the washrooms for a strip wash. Ten minutes later I found myself filing into the dining room in eager anticipation of a good breakfast. I was not disappointed! I'm definitely going to like it here, I thought quietly to myself.

The lads on my table were speaking to me now. Every now and again, as the chatter grew louder, the breakfast supervisor would clap his hands loudly, asking for silence. Ye gods! I thought. Father Flynn has risen from the grave! I looked twice to make sure, chuckling to myself as I fuelled my growling stomach.

Straight after breakfast we were off to the locker room. A quick coat of polish on the shoes and a minute or so with a shining rag saw me fit for parade. I felt good!

When the bell rang at ten minutes to nine we paraded by houses in front of the verandah at the top of the playground. After a brief inspection and a roll call we filed through the common room and into the gymnasium, taking our seats for daily assembly. Two hymns, prayers and a lesson from the bible read by a boy, suitably fortified us for the trials of the coming day.

The headmaster's announcements once again included the fact that the two boys who had absconded a couple of days earlier would be back with us in time for lunch. My new form teacher, Mr A.R. Jones politely introduced himself to me and informed me that I was to be placed in class 1A, respectfully inviting me to join him for double English with the rest of the class in one of the temporary classrooms at the rear of the gym. The original classroom block had burnt down some weeks before I arrived. Yes, I just knew that I was definitely going to like it here. The morning passed by quickly and without incident.

As we all filed into the dining hall for lunch I became aware of a restlessness creeping in amongst the boys. A definite air of excitement, tinged with apprehension and dread. I had noticed two policemen leaving through the rear entrance in the middle of the verandah when we came out from school and thought nothing of it; however, it shortly became evident that they had just returned the two captured absconders into the custody of the headmaster. We took our places at the dining tables. No one motioned to move toward the hotplates, and all was quiet. I noticed that the double doors leading into the Board Room corridor had been wedged open. No one spoke, and no one moved, including the supervising master. It seemed as if time itself were standing still!

Suddenly, loud voices rang out, echoing up and down the corridor and resounding around the dining hall. "Run away from my school would you?" a loud voice shouted in a familiar Welsh accent. As the headmaster continued his verbal assault I heard the unmistakeably hard slaps, raining in quick succession on the boys' faces and the dull thuds as their bodies hit the boardroom wall, echoing up and down the corridor accompanied by their pitiful pleas for mercy. "Please don't hit me sir, please don't" their voices sadly shouted out as I heard several more loud slaps. I could hear a struggle taking place, as if someone was wrestling. "No. don't hit me sir, please don't hit me!" I heard the cries again. The scuffling stopped and I could hear the boys sobbing.

A Whoosh and a loud thwack was followed by a blood curdling scream that found its way to the very pit of my stomach, and another and another until the first boy had received six strokes, screaming loudly as each one bit into him. It was horrible! My stomach churned and I wanted to be sick. I desperately prayed for it to stop, but it continued with the other boy receiving his six strokes, screaming as each one cut through his thin clothing and into his buttocks, while the whole school sat in silent dread, not daring to move, almost afraid to breathe, just listening to the punishment taking place some twenty yards or so away, and quietly offering a prayer of thanks that it was not one them on the receiving end of the headmasters cane.

It was nothing more than a licensed flogging. "You want to run, do you?" He screamed at them, "You want to run!" "No sir, no sir" they cried as one, still sobbing from that terrible beating. "You can run alright" he shouted as he and the P.E. master frogmarched them out into the playground and set them off on an afternoon of laps, under the watchful eye of yet another master.

The headmaster marched up to the dining hall entrance and adopted a menacing stance, his stout body erect, red faced, sweating and boiling with rage. His jacket was off now, the sleeves of his white shirt rolled up above the elbow, his waistcoat unbuttoned. His blazing eyes defiantly surveyed the sea of frightened faces for a few seconds as he stood there, square on in the doorway with his legs slightly apart, his elbows bent, and his clenched fists raised to waist height, still clutching the long bamboo cane in his right hand, reminiscent of a circus strongman displaying his muscles to a gawping public.

After what seemed like an eternity he turned and left, saying nothing as his leather soled brogues clip clopped back down the corridor and into his inner sanctum, the board room, slamming the door behind him. The dining hall supervisor, his face stern and obviously concerned motioned silently with a short wave of his left hand to two boys sitting near the doors. They removed the wedges and the doors swung shut. We filed to the hotplates to collect our meals, eating in silence after we had said grace. Maybe I would not like it here after all, I quietly thought to myself.

We paraded once more in front of the verandah in preparation for the afternoon lessons. It was a little before two o clock. The two boys continued to lap the playground, dragging their feet and stumbling occasionally as the schools compliment looked on. It was a pitiful sight indeed, a pitiful sight! I had no way of knowing at the time that in just a few short weeks it would be me out there, running, tripping, staggering and stumbling, fighting back the tears as I attempted to dodge yet another swipe of the cane by picking up speed as I passed the headmaster where he had stationed himself at the door of the bottom entrance to the washroom corridor, wondering when, and if, my torment would ever come to an end!

The rest of the afternoon passed without incident, and, as we piled into the playground after school for a quick game of football before the evening meal, I saw that the two unfortunate souls were still there. They were staggering now, much slower than before, exhausted, totally spent, their arms pathetically flapping from side to side as they struggled to keep up some sort of pace. Their tears had left tracks of dirty lines as they ran down their blood red cheeks, and, quite obviously, they were feeling extremely sorry for themselves. The headmaster, thankfully, called them from their torture. After a quick finger wagging and a loud rebuke he sent them to wash and allowed them to take their places with the rest of us as we excitedly filed into the dining hall in anticipation of yet another fine meal.

Brynn Williams was a small but stocky man with a strong look about him, thin on top with wisps of silky white hair neatly brushed back in an attempt to conceal as much of his shiny scalp as was humanly possible without the purchase of a toupee! He projected his voice very well, not surprisingly because he had spent a large part of his youth actively involved in repertory theatre. In addition to his duties as Quorn housemaster, he managed the school drama class. He was generally very popular with the boys, especially the members of Quorn, despite his quickfire temper that could see him turn on you in an instant. He was destined to be the first of many approved school masters to vent their displeasure on me physically.

I sat quietly and obediently through the house meeting listening to the usual guff of the chairman's address about sports, election of councillors, the number of house points awarded or deducted, the reasons why, and who was on this weeks haircut list. The chairman, a boy elected by the rest of the house welcomed me to Quorn, wished me good luck during my stay here and informed me that I would continue with the toilet cleaning as my daily chore for the rest of the term.

When all of the business had been discussed we played games, read comics or just sat and chatted amongst ourselves. This gave me my first real opportunity to get to know some of the boys, giving me a chance to foster a few friendships. I enjoyed the evening, especially the bit where I found out that I would be receiving one and threepence pocket money every Friday and that I would be allowed to spend this princely sum in the Tuck shop on Saturday. I left for supper very much looking forward to the next house meeting.

We met again after supper for vespers. These were evening prayers that we said together as a house. To Brynn Williams, and to every other housemaster for that matter, it was a very serious affair; to me however, it was nothing more than a big joke that was about to blow up in my face, literally!

My new found friend, Billy Brown was standing next to me in the back row as Mr Williams conducted the prayers. Prior to vespers I had been telling him one of my famous dirty filthy little jokes, as Father Flynn had put it, all those years ago. Vespers had interrupted the telling of my story, so, tittering away to myself I decided to continue in quiet opposition to Mr Williams. I was so full of myself, eyes shut, hands clasped firmly in front of me as I rudely whispered my story to the tittering Billy that I neither heard nor saw the approaching housemaster.

I saw stars as his enormously strong arm knocked me clean off my feet with a single swipe, sending me tumbling unceremoniously to the floor. He screamed loudly as he picked me back up by the collar of my shirt with one hand and slapped me from side to side with the other. He was like a demon, possessed "How dare you?" he screamed at me several times as he continued to slap the living daylights out me. "You insolent young whippersnapper!" he screeched as he hit me time and time again. His great eyes bulged and his face went purple with rage. Never before had I underestimated a man so badly! He threw me to the ground, screaming. "Get out of here you insolent pig! Get out!" I staggered through the door of the common room, weeping as I held my head in my hands to hide my shame, the taste of blood thick in my mouth from the bloody nose and fat lip that I had just received.

By the time I had cleaned myself up it was time for bed. I followed the rest of the boys up to the dormitories, undressed, and lay quietly in my bed, holding back the tears as I considered the events of the day. I most definitely did not like it here!

Although very tired, I found it difficult to drop off to sleep that night. The events of this terrible day were still very much at the forefront of my mind. I lay back, staring at the night light, wondering just how it had all come down to this. I looked back again at the events in my young life that had reduced me to the status of a human punch bag, and found myself wandering once again through the ruins of the bombed out houses in Conybere Street, in the company of my best friend, Stephen Phillips. It was the day that Father Flynn had died.

NINE

Running Away from Home, Again!

"Is that your Loll up there, Felvy?" Steve asked. He chuckled away as he pointed across the piles of rubble to a dangerously crumbling chimney on the side of a derelict house. I had to look twice. Lawrence was perched halfway up on a parapet of loose bricks. He was wearing a very old style gas mask with two protruding glass lenses mounted in the rubber face piece that was attached to his head with a network of black rubber crossover straps. An enormously long black rubber concertina style breathing tube with a black filter box on the end was attached to the mouthpiece as he bellowed and strutted around on his platform, pretending he was an elephant.

We stood out of sight in the rubble, just watching him as he paraded to and fro along the parapet, both arms at full stretch, his hands holding the end of his makeshift trunk as he moved it up and down, bellowing at the top of his voice, completely oblivious to the fact that he was not alone. We laughed quietly at his squeaky attempts at mimicry, though we both conceded that the echo of his voice down the tube did give his efforts more than just a little credibility.

"Oi! Loll!" Steve shouted at him. Lawrence visibly

shook as he looked down at us, removing his gas mask to reveal a rather embarrassed face. "Your David's just killed a priest!" "Fuck off" retorted Lawrence, "I don't believe you!" "He has, honest" whined Steve. "Father Flynn; and I was with him!" "Is that right Dave" he said in his broad Brummie accent as he began to climb down to us. "No, he would have died anyway". "What do mean? Is he really dead?" he inquired, "You know, proper dead". "Oh yeah, he's dead alright. He collapsed in the school playground".

I explained all the gory details of the episode in the playground, and my subsequent caning by Mr Preece as he listened with great interest. "What are you going to do now?" he asked with more than just a hint of concern. "We are running away from home" Steve blurted out. "Really! Can I come?" Lawrence asked excitedly. "I've never run away from home before!"

It was beginning to cloud over now. The rain was well on its way but it was still quite warm. We listened to the gentle rumble of the distant thunder as we casually picked our way through the derelict houses looking for the most comfortable shelter we could possibly find. As the sky grew darker the sound of the thunder grew louder. Spatters of rain fell from the evening sky, a timely warning that we must hasten our efforts or risk a soaking. The wind picked up and the rain began to beat down on us as we ran through an old courtyard of crumbling terraced houses, past the padlocked brew-house and through the first open door we could see. A veritable palace!

We guessed that this house had not been empty for very long. It still had a certain warmth about it, probably because no one had smashed the windows or ripped the front door off yet. A cherry red leatherette three piece suite was neatly positioned around the room; it's armchairs in two corners with the settee facing the open fireplace, still full of ashes from the last occupants. A red hearth rug with tassels, threadbare but clean, lay on the cracked brown diamond patterned linoleum floor covering in front of the grate. I could understand why that had been left behind, though it was not much worse than the scruffy old thing that we had in our house!

"Look at that!" said Lawrence as he pointed to a brass ornamental plate hanging from the wall on the left hand side of the chimney breast. We looked on at the embossed brass relief of the Golden Hind, shining as if it had been polished just minutes before. "That reminds me of the back of a halfpenny" Steve said thoughtfully. We all agreed. "I wonder if they left anything in this old sideboard?" mused Lawrence as he slid open the drawer, "Or even the Gas meter!" The drawer was full of bits and pieces, cottons, buttons, needles, knitting pins and the like, not an unusual find at all. "Try the cupboard Loll" I shouted. He pulled open the door without much effort and began to rummage around for anything of value. He helped himself to a few pennies and a two bob bit that lay on a shelf inside the cupboard. "That will feed us later on" he said with a triumphant look on his face. "Shall we have a look upstairs?"

The layout was exactly the same as every other terraced back to back house in the area. I led as usual, through the doorway, past the coal-hole and kitchen entrance and started to make my way up the twisting, creaking wooden staircase. I'm not sure why I trod so carefully, trying not to make the stairs creak; after all, it was empty and there would definitely be nobody next door! The stairwell was dark due to the two bedroom doors at the top being closed. I didn't even bother to try the light because none of the old houses ever had the electricity supply switched on.

"Whoooooooo!" Lawrence made a noise like a ghost, "Whoooooooooooooooooo!" "Quiet you twat" I rasped. "Someone might hear us!" "Like who?" said Steve as he started tittering nervously, almost uncontrollably. "Quiet!" I stood stock still on the small square landing by the two bedroom doors, listening. I could hear nothing, save the constant tittering and giggling of my two accomplices. "Shhhhhhhhhhh-hhh! I'm trying to listen!" I slowly turned the brass knob of the door in front of me, listening to the spring agonisingly stretching until the lock clicked open, then gently easing the door ajar and allowing a little of the fading daylight onto the stairwell. I opened the door a little further.

As my eyes grew accustomed to the dim light they focused on a large wardrobe in the bedroom directly in front of me. I could see the shadowy outline of myself in the door mirror as I began to advance, slowly and cautiously at first, still looking at the mirror. I could see myself clearer now. I opened the door a little more to improve my view. I froze for a second, holding my breath. My heart skipped a beat and my stomach began to churn when I noticed in the mirror that a very large man was standing behind the door, poised, his hands in the air, waiting for me to enter the bedroom. I could feel the beads of nervous sweat forming on my forehead as my clammy hand slowly relaxed its grip on the doorknob. My knees began to weaken.

Steve and Lawrence were on the small landing directly behind me, still tittering nervously. They could see nothing but me silhouetted in the frame of the half open doorway so they had no idea what was on the other side of the door. I could not tell them either, for it would also let the man know that I had seen him. The next second seemed like an eternity as my heart pounded in my chest, hardly daring to breathe while I considered my limited options.

He leapt out with a roar, pushing the door against me as he made his move. I screamed out in stark terror, grabbing the doorknob as I stumbled, half recovering, trying to turn and run back down the stairs in one swift movement. His hand caught me by the hair as I turned to run past my screaming accomplices. I shook free, losing some hair in the struggle, not even noticing the pain or the blood as Steve and Lawrence belted down the stairs, still screaming as they went. I hurtled after them, my feet barely touching a stair as the large man took chase, shouting loudly and wildly as he clambered noisily but quickly down the stairs in close pursuit.

Within seconds I was halfway across the living room, knocking Lawrence to the floor by the settee as I forced my way past him, following Steve through the open door. Breathless, but still screaming in sheer terror, we raced out into the rain to the sounds of shouting and shrieks behind us as the man took hold of Lawrence and slapped him around the room. I could not make out what he was shouting about, although I had a very good idea as I gathered more speed, leaving Steve in my wake and Lawrence at the mercy of the large man. I did not look back. I dare not!

I sped across the piles of rubble and broken bricks as fast as my legs would carry me, the wind and the rain hard in my face, totally disregarding the danger of a fall, until I could run no more, breathlessly slowing to a halt at the bottom of Leopold Street as I entered the maze of balconies in Saint Martin's flats, and finally, coming to rest in an open stairwell. I leaned on the concrete stairs out of the rain, one hand on the metal banister, the other pushed firmly into my stomach, gasping for breath, and nursing my bleeding head while I listened to the running footsteps of Steve growing ever louder as he caught up with me. I felt sick.

We stood there for a full two minutes, getting our breath back, trying to regain our composure, not trying to say anything as we looked at each other, still in a state of complete and utter shock. I heard voices and glanced up the street in the hope that Lawrence had managed to escape the clutches of the large man, and at the same time checking that the large man had not followed us. Two boys passed, pushing a pram full of coal from the local wharf, chatting cheerfully as they made their way towards Conybere Street. They did not see us.

I noticed that it had stopped raining now and the darkness of the September night was closing in quickly. We said very little as we waited a full half hour for Lawrence. He did not show. All we could do was hope that the large man had let him go. No way were we going back to find out! We were wet from the rain and beginning to feel the cold so a decision had to be made. We could not stand around here all night!

It was fully dark now and the moon had risen high in the night sky as we made our way towards the city centre. Moonbeams shone through the gaps in the low billowing clouds, dancing on the rain soaked roofs and chimneys of the local backstreet factories, giving them an eerie, almost ghostly appearance against the black sky. The gaslights flickered in the empty streets, casting their yellow glow on the wet pavements.

We made our way past Highgate park, the Rowton House where all the down and outs lodged, down Bradford Street and into the rear of the markets area before we saw another soul. I looked cautiously back up the hill at the silhouette of the Rowton House against the night sky. Its four towers, each with a pointed turret reminded me of the fairy castles that I had seen pictured in so many books, and yet, at the same time it looked a ghostly and foreboding sight. Still no sign of Lawrence!

We stood in the shadows of a shop doorway as a group of revellers left the City Arms and swaggered noisily up the street towards the bright lights of the City Centre, singing and laughing as they went. We followed at a safe distance, still vainly clinging on to the hope that Lawrence would escape and catch us up, ever watchful for the police, keeping close to the walls and out of the lamplight for the time being before wheeling right into Digbeth and making our way to the new building site in the Bull Ring.

The Bull Ring centre in those days was dominated by the magnificent church of Saint Martin in the Fields. Its tall spire seemed to reach for miles into the sky, lit up to great effect by a series of spotlights positioned around the edges of the graveyard, no more than a few feet from the low perimeter wall. Steam rose eerily from the heated glass where they had collected the raindrops. The large golden clock face in the middle of the tower showed twenty minutes to ten. The bells would soon be chiming the quarter. Worn out metal stubs of old railings were embedded into the weathered granite coping stones along the wall. My mother had told me that nearly all of the iron railings were removed from the churches and parks during the last war and melted down to produce much needed steel to aid the allied war effort.

I had been here several times before with my parents. Dad was a very keen pigeon fancier, so, while he was over the road in his strictly men only pigeon club we would go shopping, me with the important job of pushing our great big black and chrome tank of a pram while my brother Michael hung on to the handle. We would all meet here afterwards for a cup of tea in the outside café in the old Bull Ring markets next to the fishmonger.

I loved it here, the noise of the barrow boys and butchers shouting for business, the smells of the fresh vegetables and fruit, usually overwhelmed by the un-mistakeable smell of fresh fish, and the hustle and bustle of the crowds as they jostled for a good posi-tion in search of a bargain.

I always sat on the wall of the shallow concrete pond, looking at the eels. People used to buy them fresh then, choosing their intended supper as they sat around drinking tea and smoking cigarettes. Sometimes, Lawrence's mother would come with us. I would cringe as she sat there with a needle, pick-ing periwinkles out of their black helicoil shells and eating them. Sometimes she would tease me by plac-ing one on her tongue and rolling it around her lips, much to my utter disgust.

Mike and I would watch with great interest as the fishmonger skilfully caught the nominated eel with his net, then proceeded to gut it, weigh it and wrap it in newspaper in full view of everyone! It was quite a bloody process. From there we would usually go on to feed the pigeons in the churchyard, sometimes sit-ting for a while on the grass or benches in the warm summer sunshine. We had a game where we would search the gravestones for the oldest date or the funniest name. Win or lose, I always got my aniseed balls and gobstopper! I wish my dad was still alive.

"I'm cold Felvy" Steve whimpered, clenching both fists and bracing himself with his arms straight down by his side as he trembled. I felt the same. "I'm hungry too" he said, folding his arms now and shivering a little more. He looked pathetic! "What shall we do Felvy? Tell me what to do!" I rounded on him. "Decisions, decisions, decisions! Stop fucking moaning for a start" I shouted angrily. "Why is it always down to me?"

I was ratty now, cold, wet, fed up, hungry and totally demoralised for I could not stop wondering as to the fate of poor old Lawrence. It was all my fault, and I knew it. He could be dead or anything! "What was I running away for anyway? What was I running away from?" I asked myself silently. I hadn't done anything! It wasn't my fault that Father Flynn had dropped dead in the playground, just a coincidence.

It was no good looking to Steve for inspiration either. I led, he followed. It was always like that! "I wish we had not decided to run away Felvy" he said sadly. "Well it was your fucking idea" I retorted, rattier than ever now. "Don't get blaming me just because you're petrified of your own fucking mother!" "Perhaps we should give ourselves up or go home" he whined. "For fucks sake, shut up and let me think will you!" I was worried now. "Well we can't stand here all fucking night" I rasped at him through gritted teeth as he stood there like a lost soul. That was his usual defence, look pitiful and catch the sympathy vote!

"I'm going to dry my clothes on the spotlights, then we can decide what to do next!"

The spotlights threw off an extremely powerful white beam, just like the wartime searchlights that scoured the skies looking for bombers during an air raid. The glass was very hot so I had to be extra careful. Remembering the Batman films from the Saturday morning matinees, I tried to reproduce the bat signal against the tower by carefully arranging my shoes and socks on the hot glass. This did not work, but I took great delight from watching the huge clouds of steam rising high above me and listening to the sizzle as my socks touched the glass. I repositioned the spotlight making its beam shine almost vertically onto the low clouds. I was surprised at how easy it was to move them around. "We could spot German bombers with those" Steve piped up, a little more cheerful now after warming his hands over the glass.

We played away, each of us with a different light, swinging it this way and that, crossing the beams for effect, picking out imaginary bombers and flying saucers in the sky, commandos climbing the tower, Martians defending the roof, totally oblivious to the two policemen that were approaching from behind. I made noises like an ack-ack gun while Steve's loud booming shouts and whistles served as the falling bombs. "This is great….."

I was cut off in mid sentence as a burly bobby grabbed me by the collar, spinning me around to face Steve as the other bobby grabbed him. "Well,

well, well! David blooming Farrell! I didn't think it would be too long before we met again" he said sarcastically. Shit! It was our local bobby. "We were wet and cold sir" I blurted out. "We are trying to dry our clothes!" "Get your shoes and socks on son, or you'll catch your death, and then get those blooming spotlights back into their correct positions. Quickly now son! Get a move on!"

The journey down the hill to Digbeth police station took only a few minutes. Steve was in his defensive shell as usual, snivelling and blaming everything on me as we walked along. The Bobbies never relaxed their grip on our collars for a second until we were well inside the building and sat at a bench in the foyer by the front desk. There was absolutely no need for Steve to mention the earlier episode in the old house to the desk sergeant while he took our names and addresses, but he did!

It transpired that we had almost caused a serious accident by temporarily blinding a bus driver with the spotlights as he turned into Coventry Road by Moor Street railway station, so the driver had pulled into the Police station to complain. Although there were no charges arising from this complaint the policemen took a very dim view of the matter, letting us both know in no uncertain terms what stupid irresponsible little boys we were!

As we sat back down on the bench the local bobby approached. He looked worried as he knelt in front of us on one knee, wringing his hands as he spoke. "You'll never learn will you young Farrell" the policeman said to me with a hint of genuine sympathy and concern. "What will your poor mother think of all this, and how do you think she will be feeling right now?"

I didn't answer, for I felt deeply ashamed. I fought hard within myself to stop the tears from showing, but deep inside I was crying. "And what about you Mr Phillips? What have you got to say for yourself then?" Steve was still snivelling. He said nothing either. "I haven't come across you before young man. I hope this is the first and last time!" Steve continued to snivel as he bowed his head, not wanting to make eye contact. "Come on then, first things first" he said as he rose to his feet. He led us along a long narrow corridor, up a short flight of stairs, through some double doors and into the station canteen.

Steve and I tucked greedily into the sausage, egg, chips and beans while the bobby sat at the Formica topped table with a chicken sandwich, chatting away to us like a favourite uncle, noisily swigging his tea from a large white mug. We were warm and dry now. The atmosphere was relaxed, even friendly. "So young Farrell, I hear you are a bright lad! What's next then? Murder, kidnapping, smash and grab? A little smuggling perhaps, or maybe even a Bank robbery or two?" he joked with a smile. "Dunno sir!" That was fast becoming my favourite saying. When we had finished our meal he leaned back in his chair, slowly lighting a cigarette and blowing the smoke nonchalantly over our heads. He leaned towards me, placing both elbows on the table, his brow furrowed and a concerned look on his face.

"I'm very worried about you lad." I felt rather sheepish and tried to turn my head away in order to escape his searching eyes, but he was having none of it. "Look at me when I'm speaking to you lad! I'm trying to help you." I did as he ordered.

"Just look at yourself lad! You've only just turned eight years old. Your dads only been gone for six months or so and here you are again! This is your second time in a police station to my knowledge, and you've already done a stint at the little house in Moseley Road! Where will it all end lad?" He asked with seemingly genuine concern. "Approved School, Borstal, maybe even prison! I just can't understand you lad!" I shrugged my shoulders. "Dunno sir!" I could sense that he cared a great deal as he carried on to inform us that our respective parents had been sent for and that the CID would be investigating the earlier business of breaking into the old house, if they could find it. "Come with me lads" he said softly. "I want to show you something!"

He led us back down to the foyer and had a short whispered conversation with the desk sergeant before leading us through a side door, along yet another narrow but well lit corridor and down some stairs to the cells below. The custody sergeant rose from his desk and lifted the heavy bunch of keys that were chained to his belt. He was hard faced, a tall and fearsome looking man with shocking red hair. I took an instant dislike to him. I could tell that the feeling was mutual.

He paused, staring menacingly at us. He said nothing as he turned and unlocked the large black wrought iron gate that barred the entrance to the cells. I began to feel uneasy. The strong smell of bleach and disinfectant, almost disguising the stench of stale urine gripped my throat and nostrils as we followed the bobby to the first cell.

The door was open. "There you are lads" he said with a wave of his arm as he directed us to the doorway. "See for yourselves! Is this what you want?" I peered inquisitively inside the cell at the cream and green tiled wall, the red flagstone floor, the wooden bench that doubled as a bed and the white crock lavatory with no seat or chain. There was a tiny barred window right at the top of the back wall above the toilet, offering no view at all to the outside world. A steam pipe, painted silver ran through the middle of the cell just below ceiling height, giving off a powerful stifling heat. Even the light bulb on the ceiling had bars around it. I felt as Scrooge must have done when he met the ghost of Christmas to come, for I knew deep inside that he was giving me a glimpse of what he thought the future might hold for me.

Steve contented himself to stand back in the corridor, observing nosily from a distance. Men began shouting profanities at the top of their voices through the grills set in the doors of the adjacent cells. "Shut up you drunken rabble" the custody sergeant yelled mockingly down the corridor. "Behave yourselves, you drunken reprobates! We have some very impression-able young lads down here!" The prisoners jeered. "Is this really what you want son?" the bobby asked me again as the profanities started back up, even louder than before, echoing up and down the tiled corridor. "At the end of the day son, it's your choice!"

My mother was first to arrive, running over and throwing her arms around me as I sat quietly on the bench at the front desk. Her hair and coat were wet so I guessed it was raining again. It was good to see her, good to feel wanted again. I was almost in tears as she lifted me off my feet, glad to see that I was safe. The desk sergeant motioned at her to sign a release form.

Steve's mother stomped into the foyer some two or three minutes later with a face like thunder, her silk headscarf covering the rows of stainless steel curlers that seemed to be a permanent fixture on her head. She strode over toward him waving her finger as he went white with fright. "You've had your chips!" she rasped at him angrily. "Wait till I get you home!" Steve began to sob loudly. The sight and sound of the old cow frightened me, so I could understand why Steve shook with fear as she approached him. "Calm down now Mrs Phillips!" The desk sergeant waved a disapproving finger at her as he gave her an icy stare over the top of his spectacles and beckoned her to the desk.

I heard Saint Martin's bell strike one o'clock as mom and I sheltered from the rain in the entrance to the Police station while we waited for Steve and his

mother to come out. His father was parked directly outside in a grey Standard Vanguard saloon car,
smoking a cigarette, with the driver's window open.
The engine was running, just like a getaway car in
the films. He glanced in our direction a couple of
times, but said nothing. We did not wait very long.

Mrs Phillips burst out through the doors dragging a reluctant wailing Steve with her by his collar,
straight down the marble steps, opening the rear door
of the car with her free hand and bundling him onto
the back seat with the other. She slammed the door
tightly shut as she reminded him once again that he
had had his chips, before taking up her position in
the front of the car, next to her husband, still shouting angrily at Steve over the seats as she slammed her
door shut.

Mr Phillips drove off without so much as a backward glance at us while his wife leaned over the seat;
wildly swinging her arms in a vicious attempt to slap
the dodging head of their son. I pitied him. Mom
and I set off on the two mile walk back home, in the
rain.

TEN

Priest Killer

Absolutely no chance of skanking a day off school today! Mom was very strict about that. My whinge- ing and whining about my tiredness fell on deaf ears, so, after making the fire, hurriedly eating a bowl of Quaker oats and slurping a cup of weak tea, I was yet again unleashed on a poor and unsuspecting public. Fortunately, last evenings rain had given way to the bright September sunshine so the walk to the council nursery and back, although tiring, was a pleasant one. It gave Mike and I time for a brotherly chat. He was just under a year younger than me, but he seemed to understand what was going on around him.

"Mom was crying last night when the policemen came!" He sounded quite sad when he told me. "They said that you were out of control and that she was doing nothing to help the situation!" He paused for a little while, a thoughtful look on his face as if he were trying to choose his words carefully. "One of the policemen said that she was too soft with you and offered to come around a couple of evenings during the week to check up on you!" My ears pricked up. "Oh really! Are you sure that's all he wants to come round for?" He looked at me inquisitively. "They said that if you don't pull your socks up you will end up being put away for a long time!" That didn't surprise me. "Yeah, I know. I've heard it all before! They said as much in the police station last night". "Mom says that it might be the best thing for you!"

That hurt, but I didn't let him see it. "I'll tell you what Mike!" My voice was raised slightly even though I was consciously trying to conceal my anger. "I've already been away once and it doesn't bother me one little bit!" I was lying of course. It was great being treated like a local celebrity by the other kids when you got out, but it was a completely different kettle of fish when you were locked up. Three weeks didn't sound very long, but it felt like an eternity to one so young as myself. It was a long time to be away from family and friends, and the regime was a lot harder than I had cracked on. We said very little after that. I think that deep down he knew that Moms words had wounded me, so I guessed he had chosen to let it go.

Steve and I met up as usual outside the chip shop at the bottom of his entry, both still very tired from the previous night's performance. We always met there before school. "My mom says I can't talk to you anymore Felvy" he muttered with his eyes fixed firmly on the floor. That came as no great surprise to me! "Join the rest of the kids!" I turned silently, intending to cross the street on my own. "Fuck her Felvy! I can pick my own friends" he said, lifting his head and smiling brightly. "I've had enough of the old bag!" "Is this really my best friend Steve talking?" I asked. "I'm sick of her belting me Felvy". He went into his defensive shell again. I had noticed a little swelling and redness around his left ear but I had chosen not to say anything just yet since it was pretty obvious to me where it had come from. She must have copped him a real good one in the back of the car last night.

"Have you heard anything about Lawrence?" He enquired. I could tell that he was as worried as me about it. "Come on Steve, let's get to school. It wouldn't be very clever to be late today" I said, pretending that I had not heard his question. I had heard nothing about the fate of poor Lawrence. My mother had quizzed me about it on the walk home last night so I knew that she would be discussing it with his mom at work today. No news is good news, I think!

We strode side by side through the main doors of the school, along the corridor and out into the playground, heads held high, knowing that certain elements of the school would not let our entrance pass unnoticed. That was nothing unusual anyway! We stood defiantly with our backs to the wall of the Nissen hut as a dozen or so boys and girls gathered around us chanting "Priest killer, Priest killer, Priest killer" over and over again. I think it was directed more at me than Steve. I noticed the dinner lady on morning playground duty. She was looking straight at us, but chose to ignore the situation as she turned away and wandered over to a group of girls skipping near one of the classroom doors.

Terry Taylor, the school bully was leading the chanting. He was instantly recognisable because he stood a good foot taller than anyone else at the school and always wore a sleeveless Vee necked jumper with a red and white diamond pattern on it. I'm sure it was the only one he had! I hated the nasty bastard. Hardly a day went by without me imagining the time when my turn would come to pay him back with interest, but he was older than me and much bigger. Fat chance of that happening! I could sense he was just waiting for an opportunity to give me my daily thump, so I was relieved to hear the whistle blow for assembly.

We lined up as usual in classes and waited to be called into the assembly room, three adjoining classrooms on the ground floor with the huge wooden panelled sliding doors between them pushed open to make one large room with a stage at one end. The headmaster always took centre stage next to a desk and a plain oak lectern. The rest of the teachers sat on a row of metal and canvas chairs behind him, just like crows on a fence, except that is, Miss Brownley.

She was my new form teacher since I had moved into class four this term. She was also the music and dance teacher, so she took her usual place at the piano to the left of the stage. She was very often the subject of much ridicule, due mainly to the way she sat bolt upright at the piano, her great beak of a nose in the air, lifting her hands high and crashing them down again and again on to the ivory keys as she swayed to and fro, stretching her neck and swinging her head from side to side in time with the music as she belted out yet another imperfect rendition of

Onward Christian Soldiers or All things bright and beautiful!

"Today is a very sad occasion" the headmaster solemnly began his morning address to the school. Here we go, I thought to myself with a snigger. The screaming skull has risen from the grave! "Sadly, as most of you know, Father Flynn is no longer with us, struck down by a heart attack in the school playground only yesterday".

I was standing close enough to see the glint of a tear in his eye, and I could hear a slight uncharacteristic warble in his strong voice. "He was much loved by us all". Not by me. Bloody good riddance I say! "And will be sadly missed, not only by us here at the school, but also by the many good friends he has made whilst tirelessly carrying out his important, selfless work in the community". Bleeding hell, give us a break. He was a right miserable twat! They'll be naming a street after him next!

The eulogy continued as I conjured up visions of a pair of golden angels descending from the heavens to the sound of the last trumpet as they collected the soul of dear old Father Flynn and transported him to the pearly gates in a chariot of solid gold encrusted with precious stones. In fact, I had no doubt that he would be canonized and take his rightful place at the table with the rest of the saints, forever keeping his beady eyes on me and telling tales to God! I wonder if they have chips up there!

"Today" the headmaster droned on, "We will mourn his passing by singing a few of his favourite hymns, but first, let us pray for him". He bowed his head, closed his eyes and clasped his hands together at chest height. The prayers were delayed as Miss Brownley broke down, sobbing uncontrollably at her piano. I heard some sniggering from behind me. She was a very emotional type, quite prone to public displays of tears. I had seen it once before when she had a slanging match with one of the parents after dance classes. Half the school followed suit while the headmaster tried to restore some dignity to the proceedings.

A few boys behind me began to whisper loudly. "Priest killer, priest killer, priest killer" they chanted at me. That was wearing thin now and making me angry. As I turned around to confront them the full force of Terry Taylor's fist caught me square in the solar plexus. I fell to the floor, winded, gasping for breath and clutching at my stomach. I didn't even see it coming! I staggered to my feet almost retching, looking up into the eyes of the bully, holding back the tears and wondering if this would be a good time to stand up for myself.

"Get to my office Farrell!" the headmasters voice boomed loudly across the assembly room. "But I haven't done anything sir!" I gasped. "Now Farrell" he commanded. "But I haven't done anything sir!" "Don't argue with me you young whippersnapper! Get out! Now! This is no place for you!"

I could hear the jeers beginning to cut through above the headmasters raised voice. I regained my composure and walked slowly towards the rear door dragging my feet, red faced, looking at the floor, the jeers, louder now, ringing in my ears. "Quiet" he screamed as he bought the school to order. The pupils fell silent as I continued my walk of shame, conscious that the eyes of the whole school were upon me, each and every one of them holding me personally responsible for the death of their beloved Father Flynn.

ELEVEN

The Wrath of Gran

January 1960. It was a very hard winter. The mountains of coke surrounding the boiler room at Moseley Road remand home were covered in snow. The icy wind whistled loudly between the low outbuildings, turning my fingers and face blue as I struggled with my shovel, halfway up the tallest mound. I shivered and shook as I grudgingly carried on with the task of slowly transferring the gritty lumps of fuel to the hatch in the wall which led to the furnaces below. My nose ran profusely and my teeth chattered as I went about the business of providing warmth for everyone else. Bastards! Half a dozen of the big lads could have done this in next to no time. Why pick on me?

Deep down I knew the answer to that question. Far too clever for my own fucking good they had told me. Too cocky by far! The masters here did not like being answered back, especially when it made the other lads laugh, and especially when it was me. They took it personally, almost like a challenge. I should have remembered that much from my first stint in here!

"Get on with it Farrell", the supervising master shouted at me. "It's no good feeling sorry for yourself now boy! You should have thought about this before you opened your big mouth!" He mocked as he looked on in his nice warm overcoat, flat cap and scarf, banging his gloved hands against the sides of his body whilst stamping both feet to keep warm. "But I'm cold sir!" I shouted back feebly, for the third time in as many minutes. "I can hardly move!" "Well bloody well work harder boy. It's good for the soul!" That was his standard reply to my pleas. My ears were glowing red now and hurt like hell as I staggered over the mound with another shovelful of coke. "Take it from the bloody top you blithering idiot" he screamed at me. "It's going all over the bloody place!"

Pools of water covered the ground around the hatch where the rising heat from the furnaces below had melted the snow. I tried to savour the rising warmth for a few seconds every time I got near it, but I was quickly moved on for the next shovelful before I could feel any benefit from it. Saturday morning! I should be over the road at the ABC minors in the Alhambra picture house with my mates, not shovelling coke for this fucking moron!

I staggered to the top of the pile, my mind working overtime, thinking of a way to get out of here. Back down again, slipping and sliding as I went with another shovelful of coke, chucking it through the hatch and making my way back up again, repeating the process over and over again, just like a robot. The pile of coke just did not seem to go down, yet the hatch was almost overflowing. I was shivering uncontrollably now. This twat is going to kill me, I silently thought to myself. I pleaded with him again to let me go inside and rest in the warm for a few minutes, but as usual, my pleas fell on deaf ears.

I climbed to the top of the mound just one last time, and threw my shovel onto the ground below me in front of the hatch. "What are you doing Farrell?" the master screamed at me. "Pick it up!" he shouted. "Good king Wenceslas looked out" I began to sing at the top of my voice as I stood smartly to attention at the top of the mound. My baggy shorts flapped in the wind as it drove tiny snowflakes into my face, forcing me to squint as I shivered and shook my way through the carol. "On the feast of Stephen". "Pick that fucking shovel up!" he screamed at me. Bollocks to him! I don't give a shit any more! "When the snow lay round about!" "I'm fucking warning you Farrell! Pick it up! "Deep and crisp and even!"

He started towards me, half running, and half sliding up the mound. I had only just started the next line when he gave me one almighty swipe around my frozen right ear, bringing fresh pain to the misery of it all, and sending me sprawling down the slope and onto the ground below, scraping my hands, knees and face as I fell. I staggered to my feet and began again through stifled tears. "Brightly shone the moon that night, though the frost was cruel". "You're taking the fucking piss out of me Farrell" he screamed as he hurtled back down the slope to me. Another swipe across the face sent me reeling towards the hatch. He was on me in an instant, picking me up by the hair and dragging me to the headmaster's office in the main building, slapping, punching, ranting and raving at me as he went. He threw me up the wall with such force that it took my breath and made my nose bleed. I slumped to the floor, gasping for air and groaning as the headmaster appeared from his office, wondering what all the noise was about.

He lifted me up by the scruff of my neck. He could see I was really hurt. He rounded on the master, his face like thunder. "What the hell have you done?" he rasped. "He was singing sir!" "Singing! Is this what my boys get for bloody singing?" he retorted. "He is supposed to be in our bloody care! Get the nurse while I take him to sick bay!" "But sir! You don't understand" the master tried to explain. "Just get the damn nurse will you" the headmaster interrupted loudly as I leaned against the wall continuing to groan, smirking inside and, despite the pain, feeling quite contented with myself. I'll show that bastard! I'll get my own back!

It had taken an unusually long time for the police to investigate the break-in to the old house. Lawrence had somehow escaped his assailant with no more than a well deserved good hiding and the fright of his life. Oh well! It could have been much worse. It might have been me!

Since the occupier had not bothered to report the situation, the police had no leads, except for those given away during Steve's snivelling in Digbeth police station. This was followed up, and eventually, Lawrence was interviewed and duly charged with this heinous crime along with Steve and myself. I now had house-breaking to add to my already considerable and fast growing CV. Fortunately, the episode with the lights in St Martins was seen exactly for what it was; two children playing, so there was no case to answer there.

As usual, I was cast as the ringleader by the magistrate and duly sentenced to another three weeks at the little house in Moseley for yet more reports. Fucks sake! How much more do they need to know? This time I was to be accompanied by Lawrence. His big mistake was taking the coins out of the sideboard. He looked at me and smiled as the magistrate passed sentence, almost as if he was looking forward to it. Steve wept uncontrollably as he received his twelve months probation before being led from the court by his smirking battleaxe of a mother.

Bitch! Her outburst about me being a bad influence on Steve didn't help me much, though I would imagine that to be the main reason as to why Steve got off so lightly. Everybody seemed to conveniently forget that it was his idea to run away from home, not mine. In fact, if he had not been so petrified of his mother, none of this would have happened, so as far as I was concerned it was quite obviously all her fault!

By now I was growing accustomed to the sobs of my mother every time I entered the Juvenile courts, for we both knew I would be not coming home for some time. In fact, I was getting quite used to entering through the main door and leaving through the wrought iron gates in my chauffeured Black Maria complete with uniformed escorts. How long will she put up with this, I wondered as the policeman took Lawrence and me down to that poky little holding room adjacent to the courtyard. Dutiful as ever, she sat with us, drinking tea and sobbing until we were taken away. Lawrence's mother was too busy working to come and see off her son, so mom gave us both a goodbye kiss on the cheek to cheer us on our way.

Good old mom! She was there when I woke up in the sick bay, sat on the edge of the cast iron bedstead talking to my grandmother. It was Sunday afternoon. Visiting time! I don't know what was in those pills that the nurse gave me after she had cleaned me up, but I had slept through the rest of Saturday, and right through the night until now!

I peeped through half closed eyes to see if I would be better off pretending that I was still asleep and noticed the comics and sweets on the bedside table, so I guessed that all would be well. Now was the obvious time to sit up in bed, rubbing my eyes with a mock yawn. "He's awake!" mom cried with glee, obviously very glad to see me. Thank god for that! "How are you son?" "I'm OK mom" I whimpered convincingly as I slowly pretended to come to, "but I'm very hungry" I said, with one eye on the sweets. "Very hungry!"

Mom left the room to organise some food, returning half a minute later with the bastard that had belted me. "How are you David?" he enquired politely with a thick smarmy smile on his face. "Can I get you anything?" Right you bastard I thought to myself. I'll soon wipe that fucking smile off your fat ugly moronic face!

"No, please don't let him hit me again mom, please don't" I cried, feigning fear and visibly shaking. "Keep him away from me mom. Don't let him hit me again! Please mom" I pleaded as my eyes filled with fake tears, my fingers clutching at the top sheet and drawing it towards my face for effect. My grandmother snarled as only she could, left her chair, and advanced quickly towards him, hurling a mouthful of expletives as she questioned his right to beat up on a poor little boy like me. I could hardly keep a straight face as I laughed silently to myself at the look of sheer terror on his face as he dodged my grandmothers swinging right arm before fleeing through the doorway and up the corridor.

She went after him, but returned a few seconds later, red faced, breathing heavily and still angry. "I'll sort that bleeder out Junie" she said to my mom. "Mark my words! I've met that sort before, and they don't frighten me, so don't you get worrying yourself about him, David!" I buried my head under the sheets in mock fear so that my mom and gran could not see me smirking. I was still finding it difficult to keep a straight face, so I did not want to give the game away and lose the sympathy that I had already gained. Good old gran. I knew she wouldn't let me down.

TWELVE

A Weekend Away

My first weekend in approved school was an enjoyable experience that started with a Saturday morning lie-in until 0730hrs. No early morning work detail allowed us all to saunter casually to our ablutions without the hassle of having to run around like a blue arsed fly. Today was the day that I was to be taken into town and measured for my suit, and I was really looking forward to it. I had seen the variety of suits that belonged to the other boys and they looked really smart. Checked or plain lounge suits for the lucky ones, complete with navy blue gabardine mac, or a blazer and flannels for the rest, again with the obligatory mackintosh and a tie to match. I rather fancied the shiny grey Italian number that one of the lads had shown me last night, but apparently it all depended on who took you to the shop, and what was available at the time.

As always, breakfast was the highlight of my day, and today would be no exception. As my brother would point out to me in later life, I was the lucky one when I was sent away. I ate! Porridge to start, greasy greasy bacon, sausages and egg with beans and a slice of fried bread, all washed down with a pot of stewed tea or coffee. I was a growing lad, and needed it.

A normal Saturday morning would include a big work detail when all of the available boys would be split into teams that were responsible for cleaning certain areas of the school. The teams were chosen at house meetings, a house councillor being in charge of each team, and each house would have a different area of responsibility each term. Our jobs for this term included dormitories three and four. It was hard work but rewarding when you saw the end product. House points were awarded for good effort and hard work, so there was an incentive to do well.

The dormitory floor would be hand coated in a thick orange wax polish, rubbed hard into the wood with cloths, then bumpered until you could literally see your face in it. All of the dusting would be done, the lockers and wardrobes polished and the windows cleaned ready for a midday inspection. Unfortunately, the team would have to do without my talents for today. My suit came first!

Well, wasn't I the lucky one! Mr AR Jones, my new form teacher was taking us into Leicester today. He was a good egg! That had to be good news, so when he promptly arrived outside the tuck shop at ten o clock with the minibus, I eagerly clambered aboard with three other lads, all new arrivals like myself, each one looking forward to being kitted out with decent clothes.

We were in good spirits, chatting excitedly as we waited for one more passenger. ARJ was his usual chatty and friendly self, the sun was shining and everybody was happy. What could go wrong? The passenger door opened, and in stepped Brynn Williams my temporary housemaster, plonking himself down on the seat with a groan and a heavy sigh as he turned his head to look straight at me. Shit! I could still feel the thick ear he gave me for my performance at Vespers the other night. Maybe I would not be so lucky today!

"Good morning all" he began. "Good morning sir" we replied as one. "Can't hear you" he bellowed loudly as he cast his eyes about, flitting from one face to another. We all knew that this was our cue to respond at the top of our voices, so we obliged in good old institutionalised fashion. He continued with a short casual speech about where we going, what we were going for and how he expected us to behave before singling me out.

"Ah! Mr Farrell!" My heart skipped a beat and my stomach churned in anticipation of a verbal assault or another smack around the ear hole! The others boys looked on in silence. I could feel the tension mounting as he stared straight at me. "I rather think we got off on the wrong foot the other night Mr Farrell, don't you?" "Yes sir" I agreed humbly. He paused again, still staring at me, weighing me up as if to say "I've got your number boy!" "So then, I think we should start again" he said in carefully measured, almost friendly tones. "Don't you?" "Yes sir! Thank you very much sir! I'm very sorry sir! It won't happen again sir!" My pathetic, though insincere apology seemed to appease him. I had guessed that was what he wanted to hear.

The drive into Leicester was a pleasant one, giving me ample opportunity to take in the local scenery and get my bearings, just in case I did not feel like seeing out my sentence, for in this event, I would need to know my way around in the dark! We began slowly at first, down the side road between the kitchen gardens and the water tower, past the Dining room extension before continuing down the long winding drive to the school gates at the bottom of the hill in Markfield Lane.

I noticed a large detached house at the junction with large gardens backing onto the farmer's field. One of the masters was busy mowing the lawn as his children played on the garden swing.

We turned left and sped on, past the fork at Botcheston Jot, the woods on the left with a drainage ditch running parallel to the road, past the cornfield on the right with a stile to a public footpath cutting off the corner, and down to the T junction. I noticed that the railway station and the villages of Desford and Peckleton were signposted to the right.

We continued left towards the city, passing the tube works on the right and into Braunston. By the time we had weaved our way through the main roads and back streets of the city I had lost all sense of direction. We climbed the hill past London Road Railway Station, taking a left at the roundabout, past the university and into the main shopping centre, and turning into a side street near the football ground, before coming to rest in the parking place outside the gents outfitters.

We were away from the crowds. I looked back through the rear window of the minibus at the high street some thirty yards or so behind us. There were plenty of people there, hustling and bustling, picking their way through the street stalls and other shoppers. "Right you boys" Brynn Williams interrupted my thoughts. "When I shout bananas, leap out of the minibus and stand in front of the shop window, in single file, facing me. Is that clear?" he bellowed. "Yes sir!" we all shouted as one.

He climbed out through the passenger door, slamming it shut behind him. As he slid the side door open a boy made for the exit. "Wait for it, wait for it you blithering idiot" he shouted at the red faced boy. "You're not listening, are you?" He paused, motioning to shout. The boys made themselves ready. "Oranges" he shouted, and two boys scrambled for the door. "You're still not listening to me, are you?" They crept back sheepishly. I had played this childish game before so I sat still, waiting for the correct word.

"Bananas!" and we all leapt through the door as one, racing to be first in line by the window. I paused and looked again at the people milling about in the High Street. I could get lost in that lot, I thought silently to myself. They would never catch me. I stood smartly to attention in front of the window, wondering if I should take my chance, for I may not get another opportunity like this. ARJ began the ascent of the staircase that led up to the shop. I looked at the

High Street again. I could be lost in those crowds in five seconds.

Brynn Williams put his strong hand on my shoulder, gripping me tightly as he motioned for the other boys to climb the staircase, obviously intending for me to stand still. He leaned toward me, bending forwards and speaking quietly in my ear. "Mr Farrell! Don't you even fucking well think about it! Do you understand me?" I mustered an insincere expression of surprise. "Think about what sir?" I enquired innocently. He paused as he studied my face, still retaining the powerful grip on my shoulder "You won't be the first to try it lad and you most certainly will not be the last! Now get up those fucking stairs!" We climbed the stairs together in silence. He must be a fucking mind reader. I will have to be extra careful with him!

Unfortunately, the blazer and flannels that the tailor gave me off the peg fitted perfectly. Shit! He was obviously not bothered about growing room. Probably wanted the custom every six months or so! I sat on the wooden chair while the tailor sewed a badge on the pocket, bearing the initials DBS. The other lads tried on their new suits and Brynn Williams continued to watch me like a hawk. I pondered my missed opportunity to do a runner as I waited for the rest to finish, and remembered the severe caning of the two absconders a few days earlier. That would not apply to me of course, for I would not get caught! I was far too clever for that!

The afternoon bought a round of inter-house

matches at football. I enjoyed them immensely as a spectator, cheering on Quorn to a two nil win over Fernie. After tea we were allowed to watch television. I had never seen a television projector before, and we only had one channel; BBC, but it was enjoyable.

Brynn Williams was on duty that evening so he took vespers in the common room. I had learnt a hard lesson the other night so I remained silent throughout as I watched his sly eyes glancing toward me every few seconds as he read from the prayer book.

After breakfast on Sunday we paraded in our best clothes, me in my brand new blazer and flannels, highly polished shoes and school tie with a perfect Windsor knot, carrying a gabardine mac and holding out a comb and a penny for inspection. We were off to church.

I was at the front as Mr AR Jones led us off at a brisk walk in column of three, around the school and down the drive to the main road. Brynn Williams walked three or four paces behind me. I think he had put me at the front on purpose, just to keep an eye on me. Half a dozen or so other masters accompanied us at the flanks and rear, quite obviously to deter potential absconders. Boys and masters alike chatted amicably to one another as we strode on to the tee junction and turned right towards the village of Desford. We crossed the railway line at the level crossing and began our ascent up the steep winding hill as we passed the Lancaster public house.

AR Jones was still leading the way as he stepped out, increasing his pace as he leaned into the steep incline, waving his stick with a flamboyant swagger, determined that he would reach the top without stopping, thereby preserving his credibility with the boys. It was hard work. I was sweating like a pig now and struggling for breath. We all were as we pressed on, over the top of the hill and into the village, around the back, up the steps and through the lych gate into the churchyard, before coming to a halt just short of the main doors that led to the interior of this beautifully decorated Norman church. Again, I was conscious of Brynn Williams keeping his eye on me as if he expected me to run away. Grow up man. I'm too fucking knackered after that hike. It must have been at least three miles!

If it hadn't been for the hundred or so Desford boys in forced attendance, I think that they may as well not have bothered to open the church. I was used to a packed church at home, all of us shuddering as fire and brimstone accompanied the wrath of God from the pulpit. This was totally different. Apart from us it was a very small congregation, though I must admit there were some pretty fit young ladies in this choir!

The service was almost a competition. The Desford boys sang with great gusto at the tops of their voices while the choir threw in some pretty fancy descants. I enjoyed it immensely. It was a far cry from the days of Father Flynn. The organ swelled for each hymn, swelling even louder for the last verse and giving real feeling to the music. The sermon was friendly and informative, and a Desford master read the lesson.

During the final hymn, two highly trusted Desford boys took charge of the collection, relieving us of our pennies as the plate was passed round, craftily looking out for boys who thought they might keep their pittance to spend in the tuck shop. Fucking snitches!

You couldn't cheat anyway because they knew exactly how many boys were there and they would pick it up in the count after the service. I had been warned about this by one of the other lads before we set out. Apparently, when it happened before, all of the boys were made to stand outside on parade until the culprit was discovered. That had taken over an hour of searching. The headmaster regarded it as theft, so it was a dose of the cane when you got back, then the wrath of the rest of the boys for having to stand there on parade and being made late for dinner. Not really worth it for a penny!

The walk back was a lot easier. Downhill this time, so we were a good ten minutes quicker. When we had passed the railway lines we piled over the stile on the left and along the public footpath through the cornfield, over the next stile and into Markfield lane, cutting even more time off our journey. I noted these rat runs with great interest. My, my! I was learning my way around, very quickly indeed!

A three course lunch was followed by a quick change into our everyday clothes, and an afternoon of games or other activities. When you had been there for a year you could go on privilege walks. These were unaccompanied walks around the local countryside, within certain boundaries and timings. That was a long way off for me, so I contented myself with lazing about in the spring sunshine with a few other boys, talking, listening, just getting to know each other and making friends.

An hour of television after the evening meal, ablutions, supper, evening report and vespers was the Sunday evening routine. I crawled into my bed that night a very happy young man. I had had a good day and I was tired. Roll on next weekend. Better still, roll on the weekend after that, for when I had been here for three weeks I would be eligible to have visitors!

As usual, I lay awake for a while after lights out. I could think much more clearly then, despite the mixture of whispered chatter and gentle snoring from the rest of the dormitory. My mother was never very far away from my thoughts, neither were my brother and sisters, my grandmother whom I loved so dearly, my old friends, where I lived and how much I missed it all. I would ask myself many questions in these dark hours, looking for answers and reasons, but as always, in the forefront of my mind at the closing of each day was the face of my father. I missed him terribly. He had been dead for more than four years now, and time was not healing my pain!

As I began to doze off to sleep, I found myself once again drifting back to that icy cold snowy January of 1960.

THIRTEEN

Reading my mind

"So David how was Christmas?" I sat opposite the lank haired, bearded scruffy twat of a psychiatrist in a small room adjoining the sick bay at Moseley road remand home. He drew slowly on his cigarette as he waited patiently for my answer, his round glaring eyes almost boring holes in my face. I remained silent, staring wistfully around the room.

"Did you like it?" He drew on his cigarette again as he continued to wait for an answer. My mind was racing. What the fuck does he want from me? What does he need to hear in order for me to get of here? What pearl of youthful wisdom must I come up with to get rid of him?

"Did you have lots of presents, David?" I hated it when people called me David for it was usually when I was in trouble. My mind continued to race, looking for the answers that I thought he wanted to hear. Do I tell him the truth? No sir, I fucking hated Christmas. My Dad was dead and all I got was a poxy three coloured torch which cost 2s/6d from Woolworths. That, and a sock with two oranges, an apple and some fucking monkey nuts in it! Did he really want to hear that?

He continued to stare, saying nothing as his eyes searched mine for a reaction.

How about me and my brother stayed with our four cousins, all sleeping in the same bed, covered with an old blackout curtain to keep us warm while mom and my little sister shared the big bed with my aunt and uncle, and just to round it all off nicely, my youngest cousin fell down the stairs of the upstairs flat and broke his fucking leg on Boxing day! Did he really need to hear that?

Maybe I should tell him that my dad's family won't have anything to do with us anymore because my mom bought herself a red dress for Christmas. They thought that eleven months was not a long enough period of mourning!

He was getting to me! I tried hard to avoid eye contact lest my own eyes filled with tears. I could feel that they were not far away. I felt alone now, isolated! Still, I kept my nerve and remained silent.

"You are a very angry young man, aren't you David" he continued in measured monotones. He stubbed his cigarette out in the glass ashtray on the table that separated us, continuing to stare at me, waiting for some sort of response. The silence seemed to last forever as I continued to think hard for an answer that would appease him. My silence was becoming embarrassing. Maybe that was what he wanted in order to get me to open up to him!

"Life hasn't been very kind to you and your family has it David? In fact, I think you have had it a lot harder than most boys that I come into contact with".

He was probing now, and I knew it! Still I continued to gaze around the room, silently, trying to blot him out from my mind.

"Why are you drumming your fingers on the table David?" I hadn't noticed I was doing it so I quickly clasped my hands together and held them firmly on my lap. He paused again, as his big round puppy dog eyes continued to bore holes in me.

"Some people say that drumming your fingers is a sign of nervousness David!" He paused, still studying my face. "Are you nervous David?" I cracked! "No sir! I'm not nervous at all!" I lied to him. I had to say something for I was really as nervous as hell and the bastard knew it! "So, at least we know that you can talk now. You had me thinking it was only a rumour." He smiled as he stated the obvious, taking another cigarette from the packet, lighting it, tilting his head back and blowing the first mouthful of smoke into the air, leaning back in his high wooden chair, triumphantly.

"Do you know why you are here David?" I looked him square in the eye. My nervousness had gone now and he held no fears for me. "Yes sir, I do!" There was a long pause as he studied the expression on my face. "Well go on then! Tell me why you are here". I sensed a hint of sarcasm in his voice.

"I am here sir because I broke into someone's house and I am being punished for it!" The smug expression on his face changed to one of mild disbelief as he began to shake his head. "No, no, no! You could not be further from the truth David." I could see that he was becoming agitated. "You are not here to be punished." I began to look around the room again, rolling my eyes in mock disbelief. He didn't like that one bit. Maybe I was winning the battle now!

"Look at me when I am speaking to you David!" His tones were not nearly so friendly now. "As I said, irregardless of what you might think, you are not here to be punished!"

I had heard this bullshit before! "So let me go home then! Unbolt the front door and let me go home. I only live around the corner!" My voice was raised now and I could feel the anger swelling up inside me. Fucking prat! Who does he think he is? He remained silent. "Go on then!" I shouted as I stood up pointing my finger at him. "Walk down those stairs, unbolt that fucking door and let me go home!" I was shouting even louder now, shaking with rage. I trembled visibly as I fought hard to keep back the tears. "Go on then! Do it!" Still, he remained silent.

The nurse opened the door and walked calmly across to me, placing her slender hand on my head and gently rubbing my forehead as if to smoothe away my anger. "My, my David, what's all this noise about?" "Nothing miss! I was upset and started shouting." I should not have been so abrupt with her. She was a nice lady and had a calming effect on me. "I'm alright now miss!"

I quickly regained my composure and sat back down, realising that I had made a complete twat of myself. Through all of my ranting the psychiatrist never changed his facial expression once. He did not even raise his eyes to the nurse when she entered the room. He just kept staring at me, expressionless, silent as he finished off his cigarette. The nurse closed the door quietly behind her as she left the room.

A short silence followed before this bearded cretin began to explain the real reason why I was being held in a building which had security locks and bolts on every door, wooden blocks screwed onto the outside of the sash window frames so that they could only be opened to a maximum of three inches, reinforced thick glass windows with a wire mesh running through them, and a twenty foot wire mesh fence around the rear playground and wooden school buildings.

When walking through the main building we were always in the company of a master with his status symbol bunch of keys on a long thick chromium chain, locking each door behind us before opening the next. We were made to write home every week and our letters were read by the masters before the envelopes were sealed. Every letter we received had been opened and read, and every parcel was searched before finding its way to us. What were they looking for? A fucking file!

"Can you remember what the magistrate said to you David?" I paused, thinking hard about my last court appearance. "Yes sir! She said that I was the ringleader and that she was sending me away for a period of not less than three weeks, but not more than one month!" I knew that phrase backwards by now. "Did she say anything else David?" I thought again before answering. "Only that I may have to appear again before I can go home!" "That's not strictly true, is it David?" "Yes it is" I retorted defiantly. "No David! You have been committed here on report."

I quickly thought back again to my last court appearance. It was only a week ago! He was right! Bastard! "Do you know what that means David?" "No sir!" I acted dumb. "While you are here we have to compile a series of reports about you. How you do at school, how you get on with the other boys, how you respond to people in authority, what your behaviour is like and stuff like that. We want to find out why you behave like you do at times, why you get so angry, why you keep swearing all the time and why you keep running away from home and committing silly crimes."

"Well" I retorted indignantly. "I came here on report the first time and you didn't question me like this!" "No David. That's perfectly true." His monotones had a sickly smarmy feel about them now. I didn't like this twat! I couldn't work him out. "We still watched you, listened and wrote about you! There are many types of report you know. We even went to see your mom and your grandparents the first time you were here!"

"You're lying! They would have told me!" I was getting angry again, and louder! I felt betrayed by the very people that were supposed to love me. Was this a ploy to get me to open up? He reached over to take another cigarette from the packet, not lighting it, just rolling it through his fingers as he continued to stare at me.

"What did they say then?" He paused before answering in those sickly slow monotones. "Only that you were a good lad most of the time David." I really wish this twat would stop calling me David! "They said that you very eager to please everyone, running errands and doing the housework while your mom was out working." "Is that it then? Is that all they said!"

"No! They said that you were very clever at school David. They told me how proud they were because you could read and write before you went to school! How your dad was so proud of you that he used to have you stand up in front of visitors, reading from a book, a comic or a newspaper! Do you remember that David?" He paused again for effect, still studying my face, trying to gauge my reaction. I didn't answer him. "However, they also said that they were all very worried about you, and that they just could not understand these lapses in your behaviour that are becoming all too frequent now David. They can't understand why you keep breaking into peoples houses and stealing things that are of absolutely no use to you!"

He paused, waiting for a response. "And then there is the death of your father to consider! How did you feel about that David?" I shook as he hit a raw nerve. "How do you think I fucking well felt?" He had hit the right button now! The scarlet mist was descending on me and my blood was beginning to boil. I had had enough of this twat!

"Where's my dad you fucking bastard, where's my fucking dad?" I screamed at him at the top of my

141

voice, standing up and banging my small fists on the table. "Where's my fucking dad gone then?" He sat there motionless and silent, still studying me as if I were a guinea pig in a laboratory! "Say something you bastard! Tell me where my fucking dad is since you seem to know everything else! Come on then. Where is he?"

I continued to screech at the top of my voice, stiffening my body and finally bursting into tears as the nurse and a master ran through the doorway, grabbing me and wrestling me to the floor as I begged for my dad to come in and rescue me. I had lost it! I was like a mad dog as they dragged me from the room, still struggling, kicking out, trying desperately to free myself, still crying out for my dad, still feeling very angry, but above all, feeling quite alone and unwanted.

A few minutes later and I was in my blue and white striped home office pyjamas, tucked into bed in the sick bay, still crying, though quietly now as the nurse gave me an oral sedative and gently caressed my face, offering me soft murmurings of comfort until I lapsed into grateful unconsciousness.

It was a full week later before I was summoned for another interview with the psychiatrist. This time he was accompanied by a very attractive blonde lady carrying a brown leather zip-up document folder. "Hello David" he smiled at me. "I hope you are feeling much better now!" "Yes sir. I'm feeling a lot better now thank you," I politely replied, still feeling the embarrassment of my show at our last meeting. Thankfully, he did not refer to it. "This is my colleague, Sarah. We want to take you out of here for few hours, that is if you don't mind! Would you like that?" he asked pleasantly. "Well, yes sir" I replied hesitantly as I wondered what his game was. "I'd like that very much".

Sarah held my hand tightly as a master turned the large keys in both security locks, dropped the two security chains and slipped all four bolts on the front door, letting us out into the biting wind. I hurriedly climbed into the back of the mini-traveller parked directly outside and we sped off in the direction of the city. Sarah was driving. "Where are we going sir?" I asked politely. He carried on to inform me that we were going to his place of work, that we would all have something to eat and drink and that both he and Sarah, possibly with a few other colleagues would talk to me in a far more relaxed atmosphere. "Will that be alright David?" he enquired almost apologetically. "Sounds alright to me sir" I replied with a smile as I silently thought "anything to get out of that fucking shithole for a few hours."

I sat at the end of a long wooden table, with a row of five vacant chairs along each side looking at the picture cards that Sarah had given to me. She sat in a larger chair, slightly behind me, peering over my shoulder. She wanted me to tell her what was wrong with each picture. Stupid fucking game! "Socks" I said placing the first picture face up on the table. "What about the socks?" she asked. "They are odd! One of the mans socks is striped. The other one is plain white." "So what is wrong with that then?" she

143

asked. "Well, nobody wears odd socks do they," I informed her with an air of authority on the subject.

We moved on to the next card. "The train is going the wrong way miss!" "What do you mean by that David?" "Well, it's obvious isn't it miss. The train is going round the bend in the track and leaning outwards. If that were true, it would fall over wouldn't it miss! It should be leaning the other way, into the bend!" "That's very good David! Well spotted!" she beamed. I was bored to death, but I continued playing her silly game until I came across the last card.

I looked long and hard, noting immediately that the sun was high on the left hand side of the picture and that the shadow of the pine tree was pointing towards it. This is fucking stupid! I sniggered inwardly to myself as I kept looking at the card, trying hard not to burst into laughter. "Do you see anything unusual on this card David?" I paused for a few seconds. "Yes miss!" I was struggling to hold back the laughter now. "Well, tell me then." I paused for a few more seconds. "The sun is on the wrong side of the page miss." My laughter was becoming audible now. "The shadow is pointing at it" I blurted out, unable now to control my laughter.

She looked at me sternly as she gathered the cards up and popped them back into her document case, realising that I had been taking the piss. She stood up indignantly, walked over to the green door and pressed the buzzer, summoning the psychiatrist. I was still sniggering like an idiot as they led me down the corridor and into another room. "Sit there please

David" she said, pointing to a small wooden stool next to a small wooden table in front of the window. "I won't be very long. Amuse yourself for a few minutes".

I looked around the room. That door was also light green, just like the other one. An enormous mirror was set into the magnolia painted wall to the left of the door. It was fitted like a window, so I assumed that it was a two way mirror. I had seen these before at the Saturday morning matinee when the cops were interrogating their suspects. I wouldn't have noticed it on my walk down the corridor because there was another light green door which would have obscured my view. I guessed that that door must have led into another room and that they were all in there, watching me, just waiting for me to do something. I tried not to look into the mirror. It made me feel slightly nervous.

A wooden sandpit containing a yellow and blue seaside bucket and spade set was neatly positioned on the brown tiled floor in the corner, a box of well used toys and different coloured wooden building bricks next to it. I could see that the bookcase was half full of hardbacks and that three jigsaw puzzles were positioned neatly in their boxes on the top shelf. I also noticed that everything moveable in the room had been placed in full view of the mirror.

The wall behind me held a large roller type blackboard, the shelf littered with broken pieces of different coloured chalks, while the table in front of me sported a single plastic model of a freshly painted

Spitfire mounted on a clear plastic stand. I sat still for a long time, hands clasped together in my lap, waiting for someone to enter the room, forcing myself not to look into the mirror, conscious that many eyes might be upon me. I felt like an animal in a zoo!

I kept wondering what it was that they wanted to see. I was becoming paranoid now, thinking about picking up the model aeroplane and smashing it against the mirror so that they could see that I knew that they were there and, that despite my young years, I was nobody's fool! I dare not do that. They would think I was nuts, and, if they put that in my report I would probably never be allowed home again.

My mind continued to race, looking for a solution. If I sat in the sandpit playing with the bucket and spade, god only knows what they might think. Do I pick up the aeroplane and run around the room with it pretending I'm a World War II pilot? I don't think so! I'd look a right twat! And I'm definitely not going anywhere near those fucking building bricks! That's the sort of thing my little sister plays with! I continued to do nothing, and still nobody came. I began to feel angry.

After a good thirty minutes of sitting there on my own I came to a decision! I swivelled around on the stool to face the mirror. I stared straight at it, trying to look through it like a window, hoping that I might see a shadow or some sort of movement beyond. I could only see the reflection of the window and wall behind me. I stood up and walked slowly toward it, not altering my gaze once, and came to rest barely six inches in front of it, still staring, not even blinking lest I missed something! I could only see myself now, but I continued to stare right through my own reflection for a full minute in the hope of evoking some sort of response. None came!

I considered banging my fists against the mirror and screaming out at them, but that would do me no good. They had the upper hand and I knew it! I moved to the door and tried the handle. Locked! Funny that. I hadn't heard her turn a key when she left. I looked back towards the mirror. It was then that I realised that they could not see the door or the rest of that wall through the mirror.

I sidled slowly and quietly to the wall, turning my back and leaning against it with my arms folded loosely across my chest and waited patiently, quietly staring at the wall clock that I had noticed for the first time and knowing that if it was a two way mirror that they would not be able to see me now! I breathed slowly and quietly as I listened carefully, playing the waiting game. I did not have to wait very long.

After a couple of minutes I heard the other door opening quietly and slowly, the springs in the lock mechanism giving it away. It closed just as quietly. Although I had heard no footsteps I just knew that someone was standing in the passageway outside the door. I could sense it! A loud click preceded the opening of the door leading to this room. Sarah walked in, casually closing the door behind her. It had to be an act!

"Hello David. What are you doing there?" She enquired without as much as a hint of surprise on her face. "Thinking miss, just thinking". "Would you like to share your thoughts with me David?" she asked politely "No miss. Not really!" There was no visible reaction to my answer, though I did notice a slight embarrassment in her tone when she told me that we were all finished here. She asked me if I would like a cup of tea before we left. "No, thank you miss. I'm not thirsty." "How about something to eat then David?" "No thank you miss. I'm not hungry".

We said very little as she led me out to the car. She held my hand tightly, as before while we walked through the grounds. There was no need for that really. I wasn't stupid enough to do a runner with less than a week to go, especially when it was this cold. The bearded psychiatrist was already there, leaning against the low roof of the vehicle, smoking. He stared at us as we approached, but said nothing. The half baked smile on his face seemed to say it all as we drove off toward the city centre.

I wondered if I had done the right thing by laughing at those stupid cards. Did she think I was laughing at her? Why did I not just pick up a book and sit quietly at the table reading while they looked on? Why did I not begin a jigsaw to keep me occupied? Who had won? Was it a competition? In my mind I had told them nothing, but did my smart arse behaviour tell them everything? Time alone would answer that question!

FOURTEEN

The last laugh

Lawrence and I were woken at 6:30 am for a shower and an early breakfast. It was Wednesday and we were due back in court. The last three weeks had passed by quickly. My mother was waiting patiently on the steps at the entrance to the Juvenile Courts, smoking as we pulled up in a police car on the short cobbled drive in front of the wrought iron gates. She looked cold and windswept as she huddled against the granite pillar nearest the gates, struggling to stop her coat from flapping open in the bitterly cold wind. She waved when she saw me looking eagerly out of the side window while we waited for a court officer to let us in. It was good to see her, and I could tell that she was happy to see me, even though her face was screwed up and her eyes half closed as she struggled to keep warm.

Everything happened very quickly that day for we were to be the first ones in at ten o' clock sharp. They would have to hurry. It was five to ten now. The doors of the police car did not open until the gates had been secured behind us. A policeman opened the door and brought us to the attention of the usher. He beckoned us to him so we followed him through the doorway, along the dark corridor, passing the small holding room as we were led into the court. Mom had already taken her place on the pews. She gave me a pathetic wave and blew a kiss as I took my place in the dock with Lawrence. A few seconds later came the command "All rise!" as the judge entered the court in her black robes, accompanied by her usual robed colleagues. I had an uneasy feeling about this. I couldn't quite put my finger on it. It just did not seem right somehow.

"Lawrence Walker, please rise." He did as the usher ordered. The judge looked at him, shuffling her papers at the bench and whispering with her colleagues as she stared over those by now very familiar gold rimmed pince nez. "After a very satisfactory report Lawrence, you may go, but let this serve as lesson to you Lawrence. You may not be so fortunate next time." He gave me a smile and a wink as he opened the door of the dock and walked out to sit with my mother. None of his family were there, again!

"David Bernard Farrell, please rise". The usher's voice echoed around the silent courtroom. I looked across at my mother. She looked worried. I stared dispassionately at the judge, and she at me. The look of concern in her eyes, the furrowed brow and the tightening of the lips gave it away before she had said a single word! I had seen it all before. These were the unspoken signs that I was getting used to. I was coming across them on a regular basis now, far more often than I would have liked. I could tell that I would not be going home today!

Mom broke down in tears as the judge explained that a further week was needed in order to complete my reports. Despite my disappointment I showed no emotion and said nothing as I was led out from the court and into the waiting police car that I had arrived in. I was not allowed to speak to my mother. The clock on the wall showed thirteen minutes past ten.

A quarter of an hour later I was re-making my bed at Moseley road remand home as a grinning master looked on, the bastard that had hit me on the coke pile. "Who's laughing now Farrell" he scoffed. "I've got you for another week!" I turned to face him, defiantly. "You knew, didn't you?" He chuckled out loud. "Say sir when you speak to me Farrell! Always say sir when you address a master!"

He was quite obviously enjoying this. "The trouble with you sonny boy is you think you are oh so fucking clever, but I've got news for you boy! You might not even go home next fucking Wednesday either!" I hid my true feelings, for I did not want to give him a new weapon to use against me. "It was that psychiatrist, wasn't it sir?" He chuckled quietly, shaking his head slowly as his eyes bore into mine. "That idiot was well taken with you. I hear he wrote a glowing report about you, but he doesn't know you like I do, does he, eh Farrell?" He continued to grin in silence, sitting on the edge of the next bed, looking me up and down, probing for a chink in my armour, waiting for me to crack. "Didn't get to speak to your lovely mother, did you Farrell?" he said menacingly. "She is

151

a very attractive woman, isn't she? Young, lonely, vulnerable!" He paused as he continued to look me over. "Sick to death of your fucking antics sonny boy!"

I could feel the rage building up inside me. He was goading me, wanting me to lash out. I calmed myself. "What do you mean sir?" He continued to grin at me. "It's a real pity that you didn't get a chance to talk to her at the juvenile courts today!" "How did you know that sir? I've only just got back!" He paused for a few seconds. "Then maybe she just didn't want to talk to you!" He paused again, searching my eyes for a teardrop or some other show of emotion that he could use to further ridicule or humiliate me. "She might have slipped up and told you about the new man in her life!" I winced inside. My stomach tightened and I wanted to lash out at him, but I kept my calm. "Yes young Farrell. You've got a new fucking daddy now boy!" I fought back my anger and held back the tears, determined not to let him see how much he had wounded me. He continued to smirk and snigger as he looked on, waiting for a reaction, something that he could use against me, but still, I held my calm.

I looked wistfully at the twenty foot wire fence between me and the snow covered railway embankment. "Go on Farrell, be a brave boy! Make a run for it! You could be over that fucking fence in seconds!" I ignored the prat. "Go on Farrell, make my fucking day!" I continued to ignore the jibes of my escort as I trudged through the thin layer of slush toward the wooden classrooms. "Don't think it's worth it, do you lad! You really think you will be out of here next week, don't you Farrell?" I stopped and turned to face my tormentor. "Yes sir, I do!" I smiled at him. "The judge said not less than three weeks, and not more than one month!" There was a short silence between us as we stared deep into one another's eyes, almost duelling. "Wipe that fucking smile off your face and get into the classroom!" "Yes sir, thank you very much sir!" I smirked as I made my way up the wooden steps, turning at the top to face my enemy. "I will be out of here next Wednesday sir! How much longer will you be here?"

After the evening meal I was summoned by the headmaster, a big man, very caring and very compassionate towards the boys. I had never heard him raise his voice nor seen him raise his hand to anyone, a rare trait in this establishment! I sat opposite him on a wooden chair in his office, facing him across the desk. "Listen carefully to me David" he began, almost whispering. "There is no easy way to tell you this!"

At that point the nurse entered with three mugs of cocoa on a tray. We took one each and she settled down on a soft low chair in the corner, behind me and to my right. The familiar butterflies flitted around in my stomach as I wondered what it was that he was about to tell me. He rested his elbows on the desk and began again, stroking his chin slowly with his right hand as he spoke. "I know that you are very confused and very unhappy about the events of today David." He chose his words carefully, speaking slowly and deliberately as he sipped on the hot drink.

I sensed a definite sadness in him. "Your mother has a new man in her life now David" he sighed, pausing as he looked at me, his eyes full of pity. "I know sir", I exclaimed with a false, but well practised air of nonchalance. He seemed surprised, lifting his eyebrows as he looked across the desk at me. "And would you like to tell me how you came about this information David?" he enquired, abruptly. "Yes sir, I would!"

His face slowly changed colour and his eyes began to bulge as I related my exchanges with my tormentor, verbatim! I even kept the F words in for good effect. I could hear the disapproving tutting of the nurse behind me as the headmaster listened intently. He looked flabbergasted, his eyes widening as he controlled his anger. I was beginning to feel quite pleased with myself, confident that I had yet again taken revenge on my serial tormentor. I never saw the bastard again!

FIFTEEN

Where do I go from here?

Putting it mildly, my appearance in court the following Wednesday was a bit of an eye opener. As before, I was first in, 10 o'clock sharp. I looked around intently as I was escorted to my place in the dock and waited patiently for the formalities to begin. There were a few familiar faces in here today! My heart leapt when I caught the scrutinizing gaze of my headmaster, Mr Preece. Shit, he's going to tell them all about the performance with Father Flynn and the priest killer jibes! And Miss Brownley, my form teacher complete with her sickly smile was sitting next to him, smiling right at me. What the fuck does she want? I couldn't see my mom. That's it, I knew it. I'm not going home again. They are going to send me somewhere else! The butterflies returned and I thought I was going to cry, but as usual I managed to hide my feelings.

The large oak doors opened first with a creak, and then a bang, echoing down the tiled corridor as the bearded psychiatrist entered the room, half turning and beckoning for someone to follow him in. I craned my neck to see who it was. It was my mom! Thank God for that! I felt better now for my hopes were raised. She looked at me and nodded with a smile, foregoing the usual wave. I noticed that she was wearing a new coat, a sickly Lime green in colour and sporting a matching handbag and feathered hair covering. I hadn't seen that before! She wore more make-up than usual, and didn't look so excited to see me this time. I was worried now. A man held her white gloved hand. Fuck! That must be him.

I craned my neck even further to get a good look at him. He looked at me blankly, and nodded, removing his green felt Trilby as he stepped through the door, following my mother, still holding her hand as they sat together on the pew. I could tell from his grey hair and the wrinkles on his forehead that he was much older than her and, judging by the clothes he wore, I guessed that he was quite well off.

The psychiatrist continued to hold the door open as my grandmother entered, accompanied by two of my mother's brothers, Uncle Albert and Uncle Kenny. What on earth are they doing here? Funny that they should all arrive at the same time; at the last minute! They sat in the pew directly behind my mother. The psychiatrist joined them. I tried to catch my mother's eye but she stared straight in front at the empty bench as if she was trying to ignore me, still tightly clutching the man's hand, this time with both her own hands. Uncle Albert stuck his thumb up to me and smiled as he gave me the usual wink. Gran smiled too, so did Uncle Kenny, but still no eye contact from my mother! I had a bad feeling about this.

I sat motionless in the dock as the lady magistrate listened intently to the psychiatrist. Nothing new there, except for the fact that my mother was now involved in a permanent relationship, and that in the fullness of time it was expected to lead to marriage. He felt that this would have a settling influence on me. He stressed to the magistrate that both my mother and Mr Smith thought that my needs and the needs of my brother and sister were of paramount importance. At least I had a name for him now! Oh well, it's her life anyway. What the hell!

I thought of my dad as she continued to hold his hand tightly, still not casting her eyes in my direction. Mr Preece painted a rosy picture of my life at school, putting my behavioural lapses and truancy down to my not coming to terms with the death of my father. He obviously had not seen any of my daily digs, trips, kicks and thumps from Terry Taylor!

Miss Brownley cooed, waxing lyrical about my school work, when I was there that is, and singling out my essay on the execution of Gunther Podola last bonfire night for special mention. She said that I was quite the best pupil that she had ever had the pleasure to work with. Things were definitely looking up now! I cringed and reddened with embarrassment when she informed the court that I would be the first boy ever to be awarded the school needlework prize; for a scabby little purse that I painstakingly embroidered over a period of about three months. Still my mother faced the bench without casting her eyes in my direction.

"There are a lot of people in this courtroom today David who believe in you". I stood smartly to attention as the magistrate spoke to me, slowly and in very loud authoritative tones. "I believe in you!" She paused, pouring water from the glass jug on the bench into a crystal tumbler, and taking a few noiseless sips before she continued. "Every person in this room cares about you David!" She emphasised her point by raising her voice slightly. "Every person in this room wants you to continue to do well at school!" Oh really! Well why won't my mom fucking well look at me? That thought kept going through my mind.

"My colleagues and I have studied all of the reports now David, and" she paused again for effect "We have all noted a significant improvement in both your general behaviour and your attitude towards people in authority!" She took another noiseless sip from the crystal glass. Hurry up you old bag. I want to get out of here!

"My colleagues and I see no reason for further reports at this time and we are satisfied that the best way forward is to release you from this court and into the care of your mother." I breathed a deep sigh of relief. "However, it is all down to you now, David! I am placing you on probation for twelve months. If you break this probation order in any way you will appear back in this court, very quickly indeed I might add, and I can guarantee young man that this court will not be so lenient with you next time!" Yeah, yeah, yeah! Hurry up you old bag so that I can get out of here! "Is that clear David?" "Yes your honour, very clear" I replied, as humbly as I could without appearing to crawl. "Thank you David, that is all. You may go!"

The court usher opened the gate and motioned to me with a wave of his hand. I was positively beaming, for I knew that this was the signal to leave the dock. It made quite a nice change to leave through the door! Why hasn't my mom come over to greet me?

My gran and my uncles met me at door while mom remained, sat in front of the bench with her man, both of them talking to the psychiatrist and a man that I had never seen before. He was a tall thin man, balding on top, wearing a light coloured raincoat. I found out later that he was my probation officer, Mr Ansell. I don't think any of them noticed that I was leaving the courtroom.

We crossed Steelhouse Lane to the coffee bar facing the courts, taking up two tables in front of the full length window while Uncle Kenny fetched the drinks. I focused my eyes on the entrance to the courts. My mother was still in there, with her new man.

"You are your own worst enemy David!" There was no mistaking the squeaky nasal tones of my gran, right as usual! I sat in silence, still focused on the courthouse entrance as Uncle Kenny arrived with a large steaming aluminium teapot and six cups and saucers on a tray. "Is mom coming over gran?" I asked with an obvious concern. "She'll be here soon. She just has to tie up a few details with the probation officer." Relief swept over me. "I was beginning to think that I wasn't coming home gran. In fact I was getting very worried about it."

Uncle Albert broke the embarrassing silence that followed my remarks. "You're not going home son, at least not home as you know it!" I was mortified. "Why not? What's happening? The judge said that I was to be released into the care of my mother!" Tears began to well in my eyes. Uncle Albert's eyes reddened too as he explained that I was going to live with him and Aunt Betty for a few weeks. I was booked into the same school as my cousin Susan until Easter. "It was the only thing we could do son" my gran interjected. "Things have changed now David. Your mother doesn't know if she can cope anymore!" My anger swelled.

"What's that supposed to mean? She can't cope! You really mean I'll be in the way, don't you gran?" I said harshly, the tears more prominent in my eyes now. "In the way of her new bloke, don't you Gran. That's what you really mean! Reminding them of my dad! That's it, isn't it?" Gran looked shocked at my outburst, and embarrassed that a couple of other customers were looking on. "Does my granddad know about this? I bet he doesn't!" "Calm down David! And keep your bloody voice down!" Uncle Kenny's voice was hard and firm. It was the soldier in him. "There's no need to be like that! It was the only way that we could get you out of there!"

Gran poured the tea as we sat and waited patiently for mom. It was a long wait, and just when I was beginning to think that she had crept out of the back door with Mr fucking wonderful, she appeared on the courthouse steps with him, waving excitedly over the road to us, smiling happily as if nothing had happened, and still holding his fucking hand! He kissed her on the cheek before doffing his trilby to my gran and making his way toward the City centre. I looked on; green with envy as mom waved at him frantically until he was out of sight before she crossed the road to join us in the coffee bar.

She looked happy as she breezed in through the doorway, almost as if she was ready to burst into song! I felt embarrassed. I didn't know what to say to her, so I remained tight lipped. In fact, I couldn't even look her in the eye. "Well! Have you told him?" she asked Uncle Albert tersely, speaking over me as if I wasn't there. That really hurt! The short conversation continued while I sat in silence. I was asked nothing, so I offered nothing! She gave me a dutiful peck on the cheek before leaving. "See you after Easter then!" She was gone, off towards the city centre, probably meeting up somewhere with her man, not even stopping for a cup of tea with us. We finished our second cups of tea in silence.

I didn't even need to go home! My clothes were packed in a suitcase which was waiting for me at my grans house. Every last detail had been thrashed out before I went to court. They even knew that I was being put on probation, yet no-one had warned me about it. That made me angry, distrustful of those closest to me, especially my mother! Even Mr Preece and Miss Brownley had been in on it, agreeing and arranging the temporary change of school. They had even sent my school books on so that I could pick up where I left off just one month ago! No wonder they had kept me locked up for another week without any warning! It was like a huge conspiracy involving everyone that I trusted. My gran, my favourite uncles, the psychiatrist and the probation officer! Even the magistrate! What part did they play in all of this?

We took the bus to my grans house in Quinton. Uncle Albert's car was parked outside. My gran stood on the polished red front doorstep as she waved us off. As much as I liked my Uncle and appreciated what he was trying to do for me, I felt totally rejected, demoralised, unloved and humiliated. I hardly said a word as we drove to his home on the other side of Birmingham, but I thought a great deal, convincing my self that my mother did not want me any anymore.

How could she do this to me? Surely not for that old man, no matter how well off he was! My grans words kept coming back to me. "She just doesn't know if she can cope anymore David!" What the fuck does that mean? I tossed things over in my mind, wondering how and why it had all come down to this, asking myself the same question over and over again. Where do I go from here?

SIXTEEN

Why I hate Philately!

I had been at Desford for exactly two weeks today. It was Wednesday. I had picked up the simple routine very quickly; after all, you didn't need a PhD to realise that every time a loud bell continuously rang out you were expected to do something! Breakfast, parade for school, lunch, parade for school, tea, parade for evening activities, supper, vespers, and finally bedtime. It was a doddle! Just like changing lessons at school. I was settling in well! No thick ears so far this week and I had made a few friends.

The schoolwork was far less than taxing and I had a real chance to shine since there was currently no academic competition from my peers. I could put up with the smart arse jibes every time that I answered a question correctly or submitted a good essay, for I had spent most of my school life listening to them anyway. Things were definitely looking up now that I had gotten over the initial shock of it all. All I have to do is keep going the way that I am and do as I am told, when I am told. Cut out the smart arse backchat to the masters, do my daily chores to the best of my ability and I will be out of here on early license. That's not too much to ask really, and besides, a year is not that long, is it? I had plenty to keep me busy and help to make the time pass quickly.

It was early May now, so the evenings were getting to be quite light and reasonably warm. I had done my prescribed chores after tea, cleaned and polished my shoes and showered. Now I found myself with a few minutes to kill before the next parade, so I sprawled untidily on a bench in the playground talking to my friend, Billy Brown. We were going to play monopoly in the sitting room tonight with a couple of other boys. I looked around as we chatted idly, discussing our strategy for the game that we were becoming so good at. I couldn't help but notice a very tall stocky boy jigging about under the verandah with a bright yellow plastic transistor radio held to his ear, a twisted, agonised expression on his face as he mouthed the words to the Dave Clarke Fives 'Bits and Pieces', stamping his feet and shaking his left fist in time with the music. It was quite comical to see a boy that size in corduroy shorts and knee length woolly grey socks.

He was much bigger than anyone else, bigger in fact than some of the masters. He looked very strong, quite fearsome really as he stomped away to the music, eyes closed with a stupid grin on his face, totally oblivious to the fact that several boys were laughing at him from a safe distance. I had seen him before, hoeing the gardens and decided to steer well clear of him, for he did not seem to be quite the full ticket to me. His huge head with very little hair on top, shaven sides, thick rimmed glasses and a face full of Acne did little to endear him to the other boys. I never saw him in anyone else's company, so I assumed that he did not want it. He was definitely a loner. I knew him simply as 'Bennett'.

We lined up in houses, three abreast in front of the verandah when the bell rang, and listened to the duty masters instructions. He stood on the verandah roof with his clipboard and pen while a couple more made the usual head count. Everything was fine. "Right you boy's" the loud voice bellowed. "Get away!" We were off! Billy ran to the office to get the game, I belted off like a rocket to save the best places at the table, right at the far end. The others joined us and we quickly got into the game, setting it up and dishing out the money with well practised speed.

"Why are you always the hat, Farrell?" "Because I always get here first, that's why!" "Well why am I always the old boot then?" "Because you are always fucking last! Stop moaning and get on with the fucking game!" "Well why is Brown always the banker?" "Because he always fetches the fucking game!" I needed Billy to remain as banker in order to win the game. He was very adept at slipping a couple of folded £500 notes to me, sandwiched between the two bright yellow £100 notes as I collected my reward for passing go!

During the minor squabble I had not noticed that Bennett had taken up the seat next to me, opening his stamp album on the table and spreading his assorted loose stamps and sticky corner pieces around the book, ready for sorting. He sat in his chair staring at the bits and pieces in front of him, just staring as if he did not know what to do with them.

165

We were a few minutes into our game and it was already getting a little noisy when I felt a heavy tapping on my left shoulder. I turned to look straight into the eyes of Bennett. The silly grin on his face said it all as he spoke to me, very slowly and very deliberately. "I collect stamps!" He sounded like a right fucking moron. "Oh. Really" I replied, a little sarcastically. "Great Britain, that's all, just Great Britain!" I ignored him and took my throw of the die, hoping that he would see that I was not interested and go away.

A couple more minutes passed. "I've got a penny red!" He was tapping me on the shoulder again so I had to turn around to face him. "Do you collect stamps?" He asked, looking down and staring at me. I could see his eyes magnified and distorted through the extra thick lenses of his glasses, and only just managed to stifle a belly laugh. Fucking hell, I thought to myself. This blokes a fucking nutter! I began to feel uneasy as he moved his head nearer to mine, staring into my eyes. "Come on Dave, it's your go again." Thank fuck for that. This bloke was beginning to frighten me. I turned to take my turn.

Another minute or so passed. "Look at my stamp album!" I pretended that I hadn't heard the moronic voice from behind and continued with the game, throwing the die across the centre of the board, chatting to Billy and rolling my eyes upward as if to say "listen to that fucking twat!" "He fancies you" one of the lads whispered, grinning at me. "Fuck off!"

By now all three of them were chuckling away, revelling in my embarrassment. Three more taps on the shoulder. I could tell that he was standing up now. "Look at my stamp album!" His moronic tones sounded a little menacing now as he tapped me again, so I chose to ignore him once more. After a few seconds I saw a shadow move quickly across the table out of the corner of my left eye. "Look at my fucking stamp album" he screeched at the top of his voice, grabbing me by the hair, twisting me around and crashing my head down onto the table. I saw stars!

He lifted me onto my feet as my fellow game players scattered, monopoly bits and pieces flying all over the place. "Look at my fucking stamp album" he screamed again as if in agony, and once more banging my head on the hard wooden table. I was stunned, almost passing out as he lifted me again, grabbing me by the jaw and shaking me. I was on tiptoes and could barely breathe as he continued to shake me, screaming at me to look at his poxy stamp album! I was sure that I was going to die!

The duty master subdued him very quickly. The whole episode could not have lasted more than twenty seconds. Thankfully he had been watching events unfold as he kept his eye on the boys through the window that was set in the wall of the verandah entrance, racing to my rescue as soon as he saw my plight.

"Frighten you did he lad!" Mr Wood smiled broadly as he spoke to me, flashing his white teeth and flicking his long blonde fringe from his eyes with a shake of his head as he looked up at me, a little breathless. He reminded me of my dad! Tiny beads of sweat trickled down his reddened forehead, the result of his exertions in wrestling the boy to the ground. He held one arm tightly up Bennett's back and kept his head firmly on the floor with his other hand, his knee pressed into the small of Bennett's back as he spoke slowly and caringly to him. "Come on lad, calm down now. That's it, that's right. Breathe deeply now and calm yourself down! It's alright now!" The soothing words seemed to have the desired effect on Bennett as he suddenly appeared to be like putty in his hands, his struggles fading by the second. I guessed that this had probably happened before. "He doesn't mean anything by it. Just stay out of his way for tonight." As if I needed telling!

I stood in the corner with my friends, worried for my safety as I watched Bennett climb to his feet and collect his stamp album. His face was very red and I could see that he was almost crying as he slowly trudged towards the door, his head hung forward in shame like a whipped dog, dragging his feet heavily through the gauntlet of grinning boys. I pitied him, for I too had been in that position before and I knew how lonely and degrading it could be. I could tell that Mr Wood also felt sorry for him. His quiet understanding words of comfort, his use of minimum force and his failure to neither threaten nor punish the boy was a rare act of compassion in itself. I admired the man for that.

Although quite shaken, we quickly re-assembled the game and started again, playing on for another hour or so. I couldn't really settle back into it after the events of this evening, so I was glad to hear the bell ring for supper. We were all hungry now, looking forward to our bread and dripping, and of course, the hot thick steaming dark brown cocoa that always accompanied it! The headmasters report that night contained nothing worthy of note.

The degradation and humiliation of Bennett played heavily on my mind that night, for I knew deep down that I had played no small part in the matter. I bore no grudge toward him for frightening me and half throttling me to death. If I had only listened and talked to him, however briefly, or shown even the remotest interest in his stamps or even a small token of friendship towards him as a person, this situation would probably not have arisen. I felt guilty and ashamed, for I knew deep down that I was partly to blame.

Mr Wood took vespers for Quorn that night. He read the school prayer from a book and we all recited the Lords prayer out loud. During silent prayer I prayed for Bennett, hoping that his troubled mind would find peace, asking for his forgiveness for myself and my friends, and hoping that he would find friendship, for I knew from my own experiences that the absence of love, friendship and affection was too terrible a burden for any boy to bear on his own.

I was thankful to hear the bell for bedtime and, as always at this hour, glad to be alone with my thoughts.

SEVENTEEN

We're off!

There was more chatter than usual in the dorm that night. I could sense the excitement as I lay on my back with my hands behind my head, quietly watching the moths flitting to and fro around the friendly night light. I couldn't make out what the boys were saying and they chose not to involve me, probably because I was still classed as the new boy. The door to the washroom corridor at the foot of the stairs swung open with a loud bang, the echo resounding throughout the whole building, and all went quiet. That always gave me a start! I lay on my side and snuggled under the blankets, pretending to be asleep.

Mr Wood was climbing the staircase for his final check on us. It must be ten o' clock! I listened intently as his weary feet took each stair in turn, each laboured step producing a quiet click as the steel inserts of his heels came down on the metal cross runners which protected the front edge of each step. He stopped for a few seconds next to the toilet at the top of the first flight, listening for voices. We all knew he was there! We could sense it!

He started off again, slowly, up the three steps to the landing at dormitory four, pausing again for a few more seconds before climbing the final three steps and standing in the open archway which led to my dormitory. He paused again for a while, listening. "Goodnight boys" he said softly. No one answered for we knew that he was trying to find out who was still awake! He waited a few more seconds and crept down to dormitory four. "Goodnight boys", he said again. Still no answers! He waited a few more seconds before turning on his heels and making his way quickly down the stairs. The washroom corridor door opened and closed, and then he was gone.

Some thirty minutes later I was awakened by the sound of a wardrobe door opening, almost next to my head. Startled, I leapt up from my bed, anxious to find out what was going on. It was Arthur Hill, a cockney lad belonging to Belvoir house. We all called him Benny, after the TV comedian! He was getting into his suit. "What are you doing?" I hissed at him. "You'll wake everyone up!" "What's it fackin' look like? I'm doing a fackin' bunk!" "What, you mean you're running away?" I asked quietly. "I've 'ad enough of this fackin' place and besides, the headmaster is back off holiday tomorrow."

"What's that got to do with it?" I enquired innocently. "Got caught fackin' smoking again, didn't I! I ain't 'anging about for my interview with that bastard tomorrow. We all know what that means!" I nodded, knowing that he was referring to six strokes of the cane! "Why don't you come with me Faz?" That was my new nickname now. "I'm going to London!" "What are you going to London for?" "To see the fack-

172

in' queen you fackin' 'erbert! What else?" "Thanks! I will!" I needed no persuading at all, so I quickly put on my new blazer and flannels.

Two boys watched from the same bed, cuddling each other tightly, each with frightened looks on their faces as we lifted the window ready to climb out and onto the flat roof of the dining hall extension. "Don't say fack all" threatened Benny, waving his fist and snarling at them. "Or I'll tell the fackin' 'eadmaster about the pair of you! Fackin' steamers! Can't fackin' well stand 'em!" They rolled over meekly and covered their faces with a sheet.

We were outside now, standing on the flat roof of the dining hall extension. I peered over. It looked high. I climbed over the parapet and onto the top of the cast iron drainpipe, holding on tightly as I looked around in the moonlight for a foothold. Benny looked on, holding my collar tightly as I slid my feet noiselessly down to the first bracket, making sure it was safe and that I had a good foothold before letting go. The climb down was easy. Benny followed in exactly the same fashion.

We walked quickly and quietly down the drive, keeping on the grass verge, mindful of the fact that the sound of our footsteps might give us away. Creeping even more carefully now, we passed the master's house on the left, noticing that the bedroom lights were on. We continued around the corner and took a left into Markfield Lane, waiting until we were well out of earshot before picking up the pace and daring to speak above a whisper.

We chatted excitedly as we hurried along past the jot. I stood still for a second. "Listen! Car coming! Quick!" Frantically, we leapt as one, clearing the drainage ditch with a single bound, and into the cover of the woods, turning, just in time to see the headlights lighting up the road in front of us as the car approached. We kept low, holding our breath as the car passed by, speeding off around the bend, past the woods and into the distance. My heart was pounding and the adrenalin was pumping! This was exciting!

We left the cover of the woods and walked a little further, hurriedly now, but stopping every twenty seconds or so and listening for cars or voices until we reached the stile that led to the public footpath through the cornfield. We quickly scrambled over, making our way towards the station at the bottom of Desford hill. We had decided to make our way along the railway lines and into Leicester.

The walk was long and hard. It was difficult trying to walk along the embankments for these were covered in chunky gravel, and not nearly as wide as the ones I was used to at home. These lines were also at the bottom of the embankments, something I had not seen in Birmingham. Not only was it hard going, it was noisy too, and we could ill afford to be heard as we passed the many houses which backed on to the lines. We decided to take our chances on the track, stepping on the sleepers and talking only in whispers, stopping every few minutes and listening, constantly aware that a train may come at any time.

We had been travelling along the lines for a good

half hour before we heard the first train, chugging away in the distance. We stopped, listening carefully as the chugging grew louder. I could tell that it was travelling towards Leicester, just like us. We scampered up the bank to the cover of a bush and waited. Three distant hoots on the whistle, two short, and the other long. It was a sound I knew well so I guessed that it must be approaching Desford station. It would not take long to pass us. Benny quickly put forward the idea of leaping aboard and making the rest of the journey in style. I refused to even consider it. I liked my legs too much!

The familiar sparks and thick white smoke, the hissing of the steam, the chugging and the rhythmic rattle of the wagons on the tracks warmed the cockles of my heart. It was a goods train, its freight wagons piled high with coal. I watched with affection as it passed, staying well out of sight until the rear lights of the guards van had disappeared into the distance. We scrambled back down to the track and continued on our way. Within twenty minutes another train approached, this time travelling in the opposite direction. We climbed the bank as before, waiting patiently for it to pass us by before climbing back down and continuing on our journey. They were the only trains to pass that night.

It was almost dawn as we picked our way through the darkness of the red and blue brick smoke blackened tunnels that led into London Road Station. We paused for a while, straining our eyes as we peered through the eerie yellowing half light surveying the platforms, looking and listening for some sort of life or movement. Not a single soul stirred. We advanced slowly along the inside edge of the platform, staying under cover of the darkest shadows until we found a suitable hiding place behind a pile of mail bags on a trolley. All was quiet. We waited.

The station gradually came to life, first with a porter pushing his overloaded squeaking clanking sack truck toward the stairs, then a couple of early morning travellers struggling down the steep staircase with their luggage. A few more commuters and the station began to fill, slowly at first, then bursting into life as the station announcers voice echoed along the platform, informing us all that the next train on this platform was the 6:55 to London Paddington.

We were in luck! It could have not worked out any better than this. Slowly and slyly, we crept up the side of the platform as the train pulled in, mingling with the crowds while we waited for the doors to open. No one had noticed us. So far, so good! "The duty master will be waking the boys about now Benny!" "Too fackin' bad mate! Once we are on this fackin' train we are home and dry! Fack 'em!" That was what I wanted to hear.

The crowd rushed forward, opening the doors and piling in, looking for the best seats. We joined them, taking the rear pair of seats at the back of a second class carriage, directly in front of the toilet and opposite the luggage rack, facing forward. We were towards the rear of the train. This would give us ample opportunity to spot an inspector checking the tickets, provided that he got on at the front!

The train pulled off with a jerk; slowly at first as the old steam engine struggled to take up the weight of the carriages, chugging its way out of the station, through a series of dark tunnels before bursting out into the brilliant early morning sunshine. Gradually, it picked up speed as it raced through the Leicestershire countryside toward London. Chuggety chug, chuggety chug, chuggety chug! The train sang its rhythmic song to me, louder and louder as we sped on towards our destination, taking in the view, chatting quietly and excitedly, but all the time looking for the Navy Blue uniform and gold banded hat of the ticket inspector. Although very tired now, we both knew that we must not fall asleep on the train, for this would result in our discovery by the ticket inspector and immediate capture!

We must have been travelling more than an hour when I spotted him! I stood up and made my way to the toilet. Benny followed me, locking the door behind him. "What the fuck do we do now?" I asked, the panic beginning to show in my voice. "Don't worry Faz, leave it all to me! I'm a fackin' expert! I've done this loads of fackin' times" he whispered. "Get yourself a quick wash and just leave the rest to me!"

Benny was far more confident than I, so I let him get on with it, taking the opportunity to clean up as he had suggested. The wait was agonizing. I froze when the inspector knocked the door. The butterflies were back, stronger than ever before. The inspector knocked again. My stomach churned. "Tickets please!" The voice on the other side of the door sounded old. "Tickets please!" Benny said nothing, sitting proudly on the toilet seat and grinning broadly at me as he put his finger to his lips, motioning for me to stay silent. He was enjoying this. I guessed that he had done it before! I was frightened to death! "Tickets please!" the inspector asked again. "Is there anyone in there?" he asked as he tried the door.

"'Ang on a bit mate! Can't a bloke 'ave a decent shit in peace!" Benny sounded very convincing. "Fackin' liberty!" "I'm very sorry sir, but I really do have to see your ticket." The inspector apologised. "Well you'll just 'ave to come back when I've fackin' finished then, won't you!" "Most people in your position sir simply slide the ticket under the door so that I can check it!" "Well you can forget that", Benny retorted. "You could be anybody!" There was a short pause. "I'm very sorry sir! I'll be back in about ten minutes! Will that be alright?" "Fackin' liberty" Benny repeated. "Make it fifteen!" "Very good sir, fifteen minutes then!" We listened with bated breath as we heard the inspector open the heavy door and make his way into the next carriage, slamming the door behind him. I breathed a sigh of relief. Benny burst out laughing. "Come on then let's get out of here."

We moved towards the front of the train, taking up a couple of spare seats, this time, facing the rear. Once more, we kept our eyes peeled for the ticket inspector. We watched, giggling nervously, as true to form, and about a quarter of an hour later he appeared at the toilet door looking at his fob watch and knocking. We moved into the next toilet and waited, quietly, stifling the laughter as we locked the door behind us.

A good half hour had passed before the train stopped at a station, en-route. We listened in silence to the doors opening and slamming shut again as passengers got off and more got on, and then a minute more before we could summon the courage to slowly open the door. I looked through the gap and poked my head out first, just in time to see the inspector walking along the platform on his way out of the station. The ruse had worked this time.

We went back to our original seats, chattering excitedly, laughing about the ticket inspector and pointing out the sights, the rivers, the farmhouses and the rolling tree lined hills. I had not felt so happy for a long time, and slowly, as the train sang its rhythmic tune to me and the warm sunlight heated the carriage, tiredness began to overwhelm me. Once more, I found myself in another place, in another time, dreaming of the way things used to be.

EIGHTEEN

Toby

One of the fondest memories of my father, and I still cherish it to this day, was the sight of his grinning face as he strode up the entry carrying an open cardboard box full of straw. It was August 8th 1958, my seventh birthday. I knew that that he had gone out to fetch a special present for me but I did not know what, so I lay in wait for him on the roof of our pigeon pen, in eager anticipation. It was about midday, the warm summer sun burning my back as I lay as flat as I could, hoping to conceal myself and leap out at him at the very last second. It didn't work, for he was a tall man and spotted me on the sloping roof immediately, raising his right fist high in the air and shouting to me excitedly as he continued up the entry.

I leapt down and ran to meet him, but he lifted the box high above his head with both hands, not allowing me to see inside it until we reached the sanctuary of our living room. Mom was just serving a cheese salad for lunch. Dad placed the box very carefully under the window and folded the flaps shut. Lunch came first, so I sat at the table, waiting excitedly for what seemed like an eternity! Mom further extended lunch by producing a pink blancmange in a glass rabbit mould for pudding. She effortlessly emptied the mould onto a plate without breaking the rabbit, a notable feat in itself. We tucked in. I waited.

I played the ritual guessing game with dad as we all sat around the table. He was giving nothing away, and I hadn't got a clue what was in the box. Mom looked on knowingly, Mike looked as eager as me, and Bernie didn't give a hoot as she messily fed herself the pink blancmange whilst strapped in the old wooden high chair.

"The box in front of you son, is a very special box." We all listened intently as dad spun his yarn, smiling into my eyes as he spoke softly and convincingly. I almost believed him! "The magic box that you see before you contains golden straw from a magical far off land discovered by captain Sinbad, especially woven by goblins, elves and fairies! If you open the lid and look very carefully inside the box you will see the straw move and slowly come to life!" I leapt up. "But first!" he shouted, waving his hand and stopping me in my tracks, "You must fall to your knees, close your eyes and make a silent wish, but beware what you wish for young sir!"

I wished that this day would last forever, rose to my feet and gingerly opened the box. It was full to the brim with the golden straw. I stared into it, seeing nothing. I continued to stare, trying to look through the straw, but still, there was no movement. Dad chuckled as he approached me. I was sure he was having me on. "Lift the straw very carefully son!" I grabbed a handful, and looked again. Nothing! "And some more son!" Still nothing! No movement at all! "One more time son" he whispered as he knelt beside me, peering into the box, "but ever so carefully now!" I breathed deeply and slowly as I carefully removed a large portion of straw using both hands.

"It's got no head dad!" I reeled back in surprise. "Yes it has, just pick it up carefully with both hands and look!" I lifted the tortoise out of the box, examined it and placed it on the linoleum floor, waiting for it to poke its head out of the shell. Not only were we the first people up the entry to have a television, we were now the first people to be the proud owners of a tortoise! I had never seen one in the flesh before. "This is great dad! What do we do now?" Mom produced a small package wrapped in brown paper and tied with string. I ripped it open quickly to reveal a booklet on looking after Tortoises, Terrapins and Turtles.

We all spent the afternoon sectioning off a small area of our sparse and dusty garden with old bricks from the derelict houses, while some of the children who lived up our entry looked on with envious eyes. Dad found a small wooden crate, and modified the lid so that the tortoise could get in and out. He filled it with the straw from the cardboard box and put two old tin plates inside that Mike and I had found on the bombsites. A tomato, dandelion leaves and water finished off the tortoises new home, a veritable palace. Dad painted a beige square right on top of its shell so that we could instantly recognise him as mine should the need arise. We named him Toby.

Mom threw a blanket and a couple of cushions onto the path so that we kids could lie down next to Toby, just watching him forage, and sometimes stroking his head as he stretched his neck, slowly crawling around, getting to know the layout of his new domain and getting to know us, in particular, me!. We all sat in the garden for tea, eating strawberry jam sandwiches and a home made fruit cake, a special treat for my birthday. It was the best birthday I had ever had, and I wished again that this day would last forever!

NINETEEN

So this is London!

I awoke with a start as Benny shook me. It was almost midday and we had arrived at Paddington station. After a few seconds, I regained my senses and we were making our way onto the platform in the midst of the crowds. We strode quickly and purposefully, out through the raised barrier, past the watching eyes of the two transport policemen, down the stairs and out into the streets of the capital. Benny walked with a swagger and a spring in his step now. He knew where we were going. I just followed.

The walk in the sunshine was hard and tiring. I was feeling hungry now and we had no money. We had travelled up the Bayswater road, passing Hyde Park on our right. "Sherlock Holmes lives up there" Benny pointed out as we passed Baker Street. His knowledge impressed me! We continued along Oxford Street, down Regent Street and passing Piccadilly on our way to St James Park. I smiled as I saw the place names, straight off the Monopoly board.

We rested for a while, chatting idly before Benny took me down the Mall, proudly showing me Buckingham Palace as if he owned the place. It was impressive, but I was still hungry. Still, we walked on,

185

down Whitehall so that he could proudly show off the houses of Parliament and Big Ben, giving me his expert commentary as he proudly pointed out the sights. We headed along the embankment, past Cleopatra's needle following the Thames to Tower Bridge, Benny continuing his running commentary as we went. I was grateful for the chance to sit on a wrought iron bench just looking at it. My feet were killing me! We seemed to have been walking around London for ages.

"Where are we heading for then?" I asked impatiently. "I told you! London! We're here. This is it!" I looked around for a little while longer, waiting for him to come up with his master plan. He was so cocky and confident that I had just assumed that there would be more to it than this, but he offered nothing. He just sat there on the bench, quietly, smiling contentedly to himself as he looked out across the River Thames, taking in the view and smug in the knowledge that he was back in his home city at last, and that Desford Boys School was a hundred miles or so behind us.

"Well we can't fucking well stay here can we!" It wasn't so exciting now. I was tired, bored and hungry. "Is this what we came to London for?" I asked. "To look at a few poxy buildings and starve to death?" "Well you wanted to fackin' well come with me" Benny said indignantly. I could tell that he was getting ratty now because he did not know what to do next; after all, he was just as tired and hungry as me. After a heated discussion we decided that the best way forward was to go to his mother's house in Wimbledon and beg some food and money. We would achieve this by sneaking onto the underground at the first station we came across then sneaking off again when we got to our destination. "Right then Benny, Lets do it!"

Getting into the tube system was easy! Walk along the white tiled windy corridors with the crowds and crawl underneath the newly installed barriers. Piece of cake! Down the stairs, onto the platform and aboard the first train that came! What could be easier than that?

"Stop thief! Stop thief!" I looked up in horror as the old lady started screaming at Benny. He was on his way down the stairs clutching her handbag. I fled after him in fear of being left alone in London. My heart was pounding and the adrenalin pumping, giving me fresh energy for the chase. I took the stairs three or four at a time in hot pursuit, stumbling as several more people joined the old lady in a frenzied deafening chorus of stop thief. I looked back momentarily to see a man giving chase. He would not last long. Too old and too fat!

I hurtled after Benny, along the corridor, down another flight of stairs, along another corridor, another flight of stairs, along the white porcelain tiled tunnel and out onto the fast emptying platform. I leapt onto the train to join him just as the doors were closing, mingling with the crowded commuters. The handbag was concealed under his jacket. I was angry now, not just because he had stolen the handbag but also for attempting to leave me behind. I chose to say nothing lest we draw further attention to ourselves.

Benny was chuckling nervously as he looked at me, grinning, panting and sweating. He was enjoying this.

We searched the handbag together in the toilets at the next station. One ten shilling note, two half crowns, a sixpence, one threepenny bit and four pennies. I kept the change, Benny pocketed the note. "That'll do for some fags!" I was more interested in my stomach.

We were off again, changing once more before we arrived in Wimbledon. It was easy to slip along the platform and up the embankment for we were well away from the underground now and out into the suburbs. I followed him around the maze of neatly trimmed hedges and prefabs that made up the estate, dodging into gardens or behind trees and fences every time we saw someone. He was well known in the area and we could not afford to get caught now. We could not even spend our ill gotten gains in the local shop for fear of recognition.

It was four thirty in the afternoon and his mother was out at work. He knew the key would be hanging on a piece of string, accessible through the letter box, set in the back door. He quietly opened the door and whispered loudly for his mother. No answer. She was still at work.

A cursory search of the house revealed little. No money lying about, but the larder was full. At least we would not go hungry! We were still eating cheese sandwiches and drinking milk at the dining room table when the policeman opened the front gate with a crash and made his way down the path to the front door. We dived for the cover of the kitchen, scampering across the room and sliding on the tiled floor as he rapped loudly on the door, taking our food with us.

I listened with bated breath as his heavy footsteps approached the picture window. We knew he was trying to look through the net curtains. He tapped on the window pane several times. We remained noiseless and still. We were already lying on the kitchen floor, our bodies pressed hard against the cupboards beneath the sink as he made his way around the back, rapping loudly on the door when he arrived.

We stayed perfectly still, not making a sound, but breathing nervously and heavily. He tried the door, but we had locked it behind us to lessen the risk of any unpleasant surprises. The letterbox lifted and he peered through it! We were well out of sight, our breathing slow and controlled now as we kept our calm. We continued to lie perfectly still as he made his way back around the house and up the path into the street, closing the gate behind him.

We guessed that the school must have informed the local police station about us having absconded; after all, the chances of them tracking us here for the stolen handbag were extremely remote. With this in mind, we knew that he would be back and that the likely outcome would be that his mother would hand us over to the authorities. We left the comfort of his home, hiding in the bushes of a park some two hundred yards away. Benny sighed wistfully, resisting the temptation to call out as we watched his mother alight from the bus and make her way home. I knew exactly how he felt!

That night, we fell asleep on the grass, huddled together for warmth between a privet hedge and a railway line in the furthermost corner of the park, well away from the road and prying eyes, and too frightened to leave our cover in case we were spotted. So this is freedom! It wasn't so exciting now! I was having regrets and wishing that I had stayed in my nice warm approved school bed!

We awoke to the chirping of the birds at first light, dusted ourselves down and briskly made our way back towards the tube station. Everywhere was quiet, the streets and station looked deserted. It was quite cold now, a heavy dew on the grass and a wispy white mist giving an eerie look to the loneliness of it all. We scrumped a few crab apples for breakfast, filling our pockets as we cautiously approached the station. The ticket office was empty, so we made our way over the barrier and onto the platform, hiding at the far end as we waited for the first train. We did not wait long.

We took up two seats at the rear of the carriage, settling down to eat our apples. There was only one other person on the train, a middle aged man with a thin moustache and spectacles, wearing a dark grey mackintosh, and reading a newspaper. Every now and then he would raise his eyes from his paper, glancing slyly at us from under the brim of his hat as we chomped noisily and chatted quietly.

We had already decided that we would go back to Paddington station and hop a train to Hastings! No specific reason at all. It was just a name that came up, probably because we were currently covering the Norman invasion in class, so at least we had a goal.

Although the train stopped at every station en route to pick up passengers, no one else got into our carriage, probably because we were right at the end. That suited us, though I was getting a little worried about the inquisitive looks from our fellow passenger. He stayed with us all the way, getting off at the same stop as us. We walked quickly, planning our escape from the station as he followed us up the stairs, along the corridor and up yet more stairs toward the barrier. Too bad if he's a pervert, there are far too many people around now. We paused at the top of the staircase, looking for the best spot to run through the barrier.

It was then that he struck, swiftly, grabbing us tightly by the collar, shaking us wildly, half choking us with his iron grip and lifting us on to tip toes as he bellowed loudly for help to the transport policemen that were stationed at the ticket office on the other side of the barrier. We both struggled and shrieked at the top of our voices, but we were very quickly and expertly subdued. It wasn't the first time that I had found myself on public display with one arm twisted behind my back and a great hairy fist clutching tightly at my collar!

"It's the haircuts and the clothes that do it every time lads!" He said in mocking tones, towering over us with a contented look of smug self satisfaction on his face. The transport policemen had us now. "And the crab apples of course! You've got reform school runaways written all over you!"

It was only a matter of minutes before the police car came for us, ringing its shrill bell loudly as it pulled onto the pavement in front of the station. A small crowd had gathered to watch the proceedings. The arrest of an eleven year old boy and his thirteen year old accomplice was quite obviously a major event in their lives, lending great excitement to their otherwise humdrum existence. Two burly policemen dashed from the car, calling the man sir as they relieved him of his prize catch. He was a detective on his way to work! They shouted loudly at us as they hurriedly and roughly frogmarched us through the crowd before bundling us unceremoniously into the back of the vehicle. The detective joined us and we sped off through the morning traffic to the police station. This was most definitely not what we had planned.

TWENTY

Dancing the night away

"And with the right foot now! First the heel and then the toe, toe and heel, toe and heel!" I felt a right fucking twat! "Gracefully now, both hands on hips, and… heel and toe, heel and toe, and turn around, and raise your right arm now, touch your left knee with your right heel, and heel and toe, heel and toe!" I was sweating like a pig as Miss Brownley squawked out the steps to a poxy folk dance as she clanked away on the upright piano, bouncing up and down on her stool in time with the music. I was sure that she was making it up as she went along.

"And with the left arm up, and heel and toe with the left leg! No, no, no, David. Right arm at your side now you nincompoop! And turn in a clockwise direction like everyone else!" It was sheer torture; hard going, embarrassing and painful. I was glad to hear the bell signalling the end of the lesson.

"David Farrell, don't run off just yet!" Miss Brownley liked me for some strange reason. God only knows why, with all of the problems that I had caused since I had been in her class. She looked at me sympathetically, slowly shaking her head as she spoke. "It's not working is it David?" "What miss?" I tilted my head forward, looking sheepishly at the floor, pretending that I didn't know what she was talking about. "Dancing! You just can't get it right can you?" "I do try miss, I really do try" I whined unconvincingly. "Do you want to be the only boy in your class that doesn't take part?" "No miss!" I whined again, when I really meant fucking right I do! "We shall have to think about giving you extra lessons after school! The big day is looming!" I cringed as she reminded me, wagging her finger vigorously as she spoke.

It was June 1960 now and the whole class were practising a dance routine for the school prize giving at the end of term. It was planned for the last Thursday evening before the summer break. I was dreading it, for I knew that my pathetic attempts to dance on stage in front of hundreds of people would only lead to ridicule, just like my first nativity play when I dropped the baby Jesus. His china head smashed into a thousand pieces as he bounced off the stage and onto the hard tiled floor below, the guffaws of the audience ringing in my ears as I stood shamefaced and empty handed on the stage. Some fucking wise man I turned out to be!

My mom and her bloke, my brother and sister, my gran, my probation officer and all my friends; they would all be there watching me. I would never hear the end of it! I'll never live it down!

Life was very different now, since I had come back from Uncle Albert's. I had enjoyed myself with him and it was great to have a father figure to talk to, but I still missed my mom. He had spent a lot of time with me trying to find out what made me tick, asking me about my experiences in the remand home, telling me stories about my dad and searching for the reasons as to why I kept running away from home and getting into trouble.

He introduced me to his neighbours and their children, singing my praises as if I was one of his own. This ensured that I was not alone at my temporary school and helped me to make a lot of friends. He went out of his way to explain the birds and the bees to me, a little more tactfully and a little more informative, though a lot less descriptive than Jimmy's explanation in the loft. This formed the basis of his explanation as to why my mother needed another man in her life, though truthfully, I can't say that I found it very convincing.

Through all of these talks he would tell me that no matter what I might think, my mother loved me and that she always would. He confided that she had told him that when she approached him and Aunty Betty to look after me for a while and give us both some breathing space.

I hardly saw mom at all these days. She always seemed to be working! The new man in her life was pleasant enough and he did seem to look after us when he was around, but he could never replace my dad. Not to me anyway! I neither liked nor disliked him, for in my eyes he was just someone who turned up with a bag of sweets for us every time he came to see my mom or take her out.

I hated it when he parked himself on my dads

chair in front of the fire, mom kneeling on the floor beside him with her head in his lap, cooing just like one of my dad's pigeons as he gently caressed her hair. Ten minutes of that usually led to him offering me two bob to take my brother and sister for a walk around Highgate Park. I would hear the key turn quietly in the front door lock and the curtains would be closing before we were halfway up the path. Must be good this birds and bee's stuff, especially if it costs two bob a throw!

The weekday routine had also changed. I still got up at six in the morning to light a small fire; just enough to take the chill off the room while mom did the breakfast, but everything was such a rush now and there was no time to talk anymore. My sister had to be fed, dressed and ready for the council run nursery. Mom did that. Mike had to be sorted and ready for school. Mike and I washed the breakfast crocks, drying them and putting them away while mom quickly tidied the living room and straightened the beds, yet she still managed to find ten minutes or so to stand in front of the mirror, putting on her make-up and brushing her hair before expertly tying a silk headscarf in the shape of a turban around her head. I guessed that this was because lover boy was the shop floor foreman where she worked!

We always left together at ten to seven on the nail, mom turning left at the bottom of the entry for the bus stop in Belgrave Road, Mike and I turning right and pushing the pram all the way to the council nursery next door to the Rowton House, whatever the weather! It was hard going at times. We would race back home with the pram, sometimes giving each other a ride, just making it in time to put the pram away and get off in time for school. Mornings were hectic now.

In the evenings we would reverse the process, collecting our sister no later than four thirty. The nursery was very strict about this. I would make us a sandwich each when we got back, then we would all sit in front of the television waiting for mom to come home.

Mom would be home from her job as a power press and hand press operator by about five thirty with a packet of sweets for each of us, and then off again almost immediately to do a cleaning job at the Rowton House, leaving me to baby-sit again.

She would be back in the house just after eight thirty, knackered, usually carrying a bag of chips for us all, and her man would arrive soon afterwards, except for Mondays and Wednesdays. Those were the evenings that my mom had to take me to see the probation officer in a classroom at St Albans School. We would be in bed by nine and the whole routine would start all over again the next day, leaving me very little time to get into trouble!

Things might just have turned out a little differently if mom had taken the time to sit down and talk to me; after all I was supposed to be a very intelligent young boy. It wasn't to be until much later in life that I would find out that women in those days were paid considerably less than their male counterparts for the doing the same job, hence the need for my mother to work all those extra hours just to provide even the most modest of existences for us all.

Using my hectic schedule as an excuse to cut out extra dance tuition with Miss Brownley cut no ice with her at all. Instead, I was forcibly persuaded with the threat of an interview with my probation officer to give up two lunchtimes per week and an hour on Saturday mornings. I didn't really think that she would have gone through with it but I had no intention of leaving it to chance. Oh well! It was only for a couple of weeks.

The butterflies performed their own dance in my stomach as the headmaster proudly announced us to the waiting audience. My legs felt stiff and my feet leaden as the class split equally, as previously rehearsed, and made their way gingerly up the portable wooden steps positioned at either end of the stage. We took up our starting positions, four rows of eight, and a girl between each boy, all standing smartly to attention as the headmaster continued to read out aloud from the programme.

We barely had enough room on the stage. Miss Brownley leaned towards the audience flashing her protruding tombstone teeth in a wide open mouthed smile, poised, both hands in the air ready to crash down on the piano with the opening chord. I looked across the hall at the faces of my family, as they smiled away waiting for the proceedings to begin. Mom's bloke stood next her with his arm hanging loosely over her shoulder, taking a swig from his hip flask as he looked on, quite obviously already bored to death with it all. Gran stood next to them, chatting idly to my probation officer and pointing proudly as if to say "Look! There's my grandson over there!"

Miss Brownley struck the first chord. This was the signal for the girls to courtesy and the boys to bow. The second chord struck, and we were back to attention, waiting in eager anticipation of the third chord to begin the folk dance from hell! Clang! We were off! Heel and toe, heel and toe, and touch the knee and raise the arm and spin. I listened carefully to the dance teachers well projected prompts under her breath. The extra tuition had paid dividends, for I danced step perfect and light as a feather. It was a joyous exhilarating feeling as I flitted around the stage like a sparrow, spinning in time to the music with both arms arched high above my head, the fingers of both my hands touching together for the finale with my classmates, and milking the thunderous applause as we came to rest, once more bowing to the audience before exiting the stage. I was positively aglow with excitement. I knew that we had done well.

I joined my family for soft drinks and cake during the interval, well pleased with myself. He was well into his hip flask now! His whisky breath made me feel nauseous as he leaned over to me, trying to pat me on the head for show. I stepped back as he lurched forward, almost falling over. He snarled at me. I had not seen this side of him before. My gran rescued me, congratulating me on my dancing. I noticed the look of contempt in her face as she slyly glanced sideways at him. I think he must have noticed it too, for he withdrew slowly, his expression changing as he put his arm around my mother's shoulders and turned to face her. She was either quite oblivious to his actions or she simply just didn't care!

We sat attentively while the fifth year choir did themselves credit as they gave their perfect well rehearsed renditions of Twankydillo, Barbara Allen and Dirty Old Town before the prize giving began. The awards were made by years, starting with year one. I was first up for the fourth year awards, shaking the headmasters hand as I received my five shilling book token for the school needlework prize. It wouldn't have been so bad if he hadn't announced to everyone with great glee that it was the first time in the schools history that the prize had been awarded to a boy! I cringed as red-faced I took my place behind him on the stage, waiting for the other awards to be given out.

Another book token came my way for the Scripture prize, and another for English, mainly due to my Gunther Podola essay. I felt extremely proud of myself, for I had done very well that evening, and I knew it! My probation officer expressed his delight at my academic achievements and my performance in the dance. He noted a significant improvement in my general attitude over the past few months and offered me a cautious reminder to keep up the good work. We saw him to his car. Yes, I was very proud of myself this evening!

We walked my gran to the bus stop after the

event, and then continued on to the Wellington pub at the bottom of our entry. Most of the schools parents were in there, the children all standing outside in the street with pop, crisps and nibbets. It was a nice evening; until we got home!

"Needlework and fucking Scripture!" "You forgot the English prize" I retorted. "You fucking great Nancy!" He lunged at me staggering drunkenly as he caught me around the face with the back of his hand. Mom said nothing as I fell back against the green moquette armchair in the corner of the living room. "Fucking great Nancy!" He was at me again, but I was quick, moving sideways to dodge his swinging arm as he lost his footing, sending him sprawling onto the chair. I wasn't frightened of him, and he knew it! I looked at my mom. She said nothing.

I could see the anger in his eyes, his drunken red face turning purple as he struggled in his pathetic attempts to get to his feet and attack me again. Not this time you bastard! Quick as a flash, I landed my puny right fist on the end of his nose, following it up with a kick as he fell back in surprise. He didn't like that!

Now my mom took notice, grabbing me by the hair and screaming hysterically at me. I kicked out at him again as he tried to get up, this time my boot caught him squarely on the chin. I shook with rage and shouted at the top of my voice as I managed to wrestle myself free from my mother. "You don't fucking love me! You never have!"

Mike and Bernie were huddled together on the armchair in the other corner, frightened and crying.

"I wish it were you that fucking died and not my fucking dad you bastard!" I screamed venomously at her as I cleared the plates from the dinner table with a single tug of the tablecloth, watching her face turn pale. I grabbed a table knife from the floor, waving it menacingly in her face, and taking great delight in her frightened expression as she stepped back towards her drunken consort. "I fucking hate you, you bastard; I fucking hate you all!" I stabbed the vacant settee several times in my fit of rage before throwing the knife at the mirror that hung on the chimney breast. "I fucking hate you all, you bastards!"

I fled, stumbling on the broken crockery as I raced through the door and out into the warm summer's night, cursing at the top of my voice, sweating, panting breathlessly and shaking with rage, the tears streaming down my face. A nosy neighbour tried to grab me as I sped out of our garden, but I hardly noticed, managing to shrug her off with little or no effort at all.

I ran like the wind down the entry, still shouting as I ran down past the school, heading for Belgrave Road. I just kept running and running until my tired legs would carry me no further. Through the hole in the fence and into the grounds of the old derelict Embassy Sportsdrome opposite the Bristol cinema where they used to hold the wrestling matches, before breathlessly coming to rest in the relative safety of one of the numerous dens that I had built there with my friends. This would have to do for tonight. I was too tired and I dared not go home now!

TWENTY ONE

Welcome back

It was about four thirty in the afternoon when Benny and I arrived back at Desford Boys School. The Deputy Head and the P.E teacher had driven down to London to collect us from the police station. It had been a long day and we were very tired. We made the journey back in silence, as ordered, pondering our fate. Benny had told me earlier that there was nothing to fear from the cane, for it sounded far worse than it was, but nonetheless, I still trembled with fear and trepidation as the burly P.E. master frogmarched me along the verandah with my arm twisted high up my back as the boys looked on, down past the General Office and into the boardroom corridor, flinging me up against the wall as we waited for the headmaster. I looked around silently as Benny stood next to me, and listened intently as the dining hall doors were wedged open while the boys filed in for their evening meal.

I felt the electricity in the air as I waited, forcing myself not to show any fear as I breathed slowly and deeply in an effort to rid myself of the trembling that had overtaken me earlier. I was nervous but determined not to show it. I listened to the familiar scraping sounds of cutlery on plates as the boys continued with their meal in silence, waiting for the entertainment to begin.

Although public canings were illegal at the time, there was no law against allowing the boys to listen to it. Judging from the caning that I had heard when I first arrived, I guessed that it was meant to act as a deterrent against absconding, so I knew exactly what to expect, although nothing that I had ever experienced before could have prepared me for the pain and sadistic brutality that I was about to have inflicted upon me!

The wait was nerve wracking. We must have been standing there a good ten minutes before we heard the unmistakable sound of the headmaster's footsteps echoing down the washroom corridor as he approached, getting louder with each pace, and quickening his step as he wheeled into the board room corridor, on his way to deal with us.

His eyes were blazing as he approached, knocking me to the ground first with a single swipe of his huge hand, shouting loudly as he grabbed me by the shirt collar, lifting me onto tiptoes and shaking me violently as he slapped my head from side to side. "Why did you climb out of the window instead of using the door like everyone else?" He screamed his question at me over and over again as he continued to shake me, still hitting me with his huge hands. "I don't know sir!" I was crying now and my nose bled as he continued to hit me about the head. "I don't know! Is that all that you can say? I don't know!" He dragged me across the corridor and into the board room, still screaming at me as he bounced me against the grey metal filing cabinets, punching me to the floor as he leaned over his desk and picked up a long cardboard tube full of bamboo canes.

I climbed weakly to my feet as he selected one, bending it almost double in front of me, waving it in the air and making a loud swishing sound, shouting as I continued to cower against the cabinets, my arms raised in front of my face. He grabbed me by the collar with his free hand and threw me back through the open doorway, slapping me hard on the back of the head as I spun around, falling headlong into the arms of the grinning P.E. master. He took great delight in bashing my head against the small hexagonal table in the entrance hall as he forcibly held me down with my trousers around my ankles, ready to receive my first stroke!

The headmaster had taken his jacket off now and the sleeves of his white shirt, spattered with the blood from my nose, were rolled high above his elbows. "Run away from my school would you! Run away!" he screamed as he marched quickly out into the corridor and took up his position behind me, waving the bamboo cane wildly, swishing as he continued to shout. I could just see his feet as the P.E. master held me firmly in position with one arm up my back and a firm hand on my ear, gripping my skull and pushing my head painfully into the table.

Two quick steps and a skip, a whoosh and the first stroke seared into my flesh with a loud resounding thwack. I screamed loudly as I had never screamed before, trying to struggle free and escape the excruciating pain. The sounds of his voice, the cane cutting through the air, the thwack and my screams echoed up and down the tiled corridor. Two more steps and the next stroke was cutting into me, my flesh burning with the pain. I screamed even louder, again and again as the sadistic bastard piled on four more strokes through my thin regulation underpants, tearing them and taking more skin off my backside with each stroke. The P.E. master dragged me up, violently throwing me face first against the wall as Benny prepared to receive his dose.

A few minutes later and we were on our way, the headmaster dragging me down the corridor by the scruff of my neck as I wept, screaming loudly at me. "You want to run do you? You want to run away from my school! Well you can run alright!" He dragged me past the silent dining hall, and out into the playground to begin my laps. Benny followed, helped along with a few digs from the P.E. master. The headmaster stood for some time at the bottom of the playground, watching, glorying in our misery, chasing me with his cane as we passed, and swinging it at my backside and legs, urging me to run faster.

We continued to run and stagger long after the boys had finished tea, tripping and dragging our weary feet around the playground, running past, breathlessly, fighting back the tears as some of the boys played football around us, while some sat quietly on the benches, watching, not daring to speak to us.

We slowed to a stumbling trot every time the duty master took his eye off us, increasing the pace only when he turned around. I sensed that he did not like what he saw, for he turned more often now and for longer each time, and always with the same distinctive look of pity in his eyes.

"Everybody screams like that first time" Benny assured me. "He always seems to cane you harder for the first offence!" We talked quietly under our breath as we continued to stagger around the playground. "You wait till you see your fackin' arse tomorrow Faz!" He raised a half smile. "It will be black and blue. The bruises last for fackin' weeks!" Benny was quite obviously a great authority on the subject of corporal punishment. It had not escaped my attention that he had casually strolled to the table when his turn came, adopted the position and received his six strokes without as much as a murmur. He was obviously quite used to it. I made up my mind on that day that I would never scream out again, no matter how much I wanted to, no matter how hard they hit me, no matter how much they hurt me.

The bell sounded for supper. We had been lapping for over three hours now, and true to form the headmaster appeared at the entrance to the washroom corridor as the boys filed in, beckoning us to him angrily as we tried to pick up the pace to run past him. Our weary legs would have none of it. At least he wasn't holding a cane now! We were still in the clothes that we had absconded in. "Get changed, both of you! Get washed and get your supper," he

207

rasped. "Five minutes or you go without!" He cuffed us both as we hurried past him on our way into the corridor.

We found new strength to mount the stairs to the dormitory, temporarily forgetting our pain, misery and fatigue, hurriedly getting changed and quickly washing our faces and hands in the toilet washbasin before going down for supper. We paused at the door, attracting the attention of the duty master and asking permission to take our seats. We quickly gulped down the fare, for we had not eaten since early that morning in the police station. I looked earnestly around for any seconds or leftovers, but there were none.

We all sat up straight in our chairs, arms folded when the headmaster entered the dining room, clutching his leather bound book and clipboard as he strode purposely and defiantly across the floor to take his place at the corner table for nightly report. He adopted his usual menacing stance, staring at everyone in the room one by one, his very gaze striking fear into the heart of every boy.

"Farrell and Hill!" he bellowed in his fearsome Welsh accent. "Stand up!" Again I could feel the buzz of anticipation from the boys. We stood smartly to attention, looking him in the eye and listening carefully as he addressed the school, paying special attention to the kind of treatment that an absconder could expect. He paced about the floor as his piercing eyes burned into mine before settling with his hands on his hips, still with those menacing eyes blazing. He rounded on Benny and me.

"For absconding" he said loudly and slowly. He paused. "You will each lose five days home leave and forty house points!" I was taken aback. All the boys seemed to gasp as one. "In addition!" He paused again for emphasis. "You will both report to Mr Starbuck immediately after lunch tomorrow. I am sure he will find you some work to keep you occupied over the weekend". He continued to stare into my face as if looking for a reaction. "You quite obviously have far too much energy to burn between you! Sit down!" I could tell from the tone in his voice that he meant for us to be worked hard.

I climbed wearily and stiffly into my bed that night, thankful for the opportunity to rest my aching legs and sore feet. The lapping of the playground and the severity of the caning had taken its toll. I struggled to get comfortable, due mainly to the endless throbbing and soreness where the strokes of the cane had left their bloody and bruised criss-crossed pattern of stripes on my buttocks and the back of my thighs.

Some of the boys tried to question me about the events of the past few days, but I was just too tired to answer. As I began to relax, staring at the friendly night light and its ever present complement of dancing moths the tiredness began to overtake me, allowing me once more to be alone with my thoughts, to dream, and giving me brief respite from my pain.

TWENTY TWO

Black Days

It was February 4th, 1959. Mom was wearing a plain black velvet dress, long sleeved with a high collar and two rows of black buttons running down the front to the waistline. It was neatly covered with a long black double breasted twill coat with a thick loose belt tied at the waist. The high collar and wide lapels were turned up to protect her from the biting wind. She wore black knee length leather boots and a black wide brimmed hat with a small plain black veil pushed to one side as she stood at the top of the path, staring blankly and smoking a cigarette while she waited for dad to come home. You could see from the redness of her eyes that she had been crying. She looked tired and haggard for such a young woman. The events of the past few months had quite obviously taken their toll on her.

The neighbours lined the entry, watching and waiting, looking at us with pitiful eyes. It was cold. The last remnants of the winters snow had all but disappeared save for a few hard piles at the sides of the paths that were taking longer to thaw. I stood at the top of the entry near the outside toilet block with my brother Michael, holding hands and shivering as we waited patiently for the hearse bearing our dads coffin to arrive. My sister was staying with an aunt until it was all over. Mom had said that she was too young to understand. I'm not particularly sure if Mike and I really understood, either.

I was looking straight down the entry into Hick Street when the shiny black hearse pulled up outside the Wellington pub. I could see the men standing solemnly on the pavement outside, caps off and tilting their heads in deference, each one with their hands clasped firmly together in front of them. Mom put her cigarette out, adjusted her veil and called us to her, putting an arm around each of us as we took up a position on either side of her. She braced herself, moving clear of the gate and turning to look squarely down the entry between the two rows of terraced houses, past the gazing eyes of our neighbours and onto the scene unfolding before us.

A tall thin man wearing a black top hat and black suit with a long jacket strode slowly and purposefully toward us, his left hand clenched on his chest, his right arm swinging slowly at his side in time with his steps. The long silk tails of the black ribbon on his hat flapped from side to side in the wind. He was sombre looking, his head held high and tilted slightly back, his nose in the air giving him an air of great importance as he moved smoothly up the entry like a phantom. The coffin followed a short distance behind him, borne by my dads four brothers. His father followed behind them accompanied by his brother and a catholic priest. There were no women.

The neighbours cast their eyes to the ground, making the sign of the cross as the coffin passed them by. Mom's bottom lip started to quiver, a pained expression appearing on her face as the coffin approached. Teardrops began to form in her eyes, rolling slowly down her cheek as she tried to stifle the sound of her own gentle sobbing. It was catching. I felt the tears begin to well in my own eyes as I too resisted the temptation to burst into tears, for I knew that once I started I would not be able to stop.

As the sombre procession arrived at the gate the tall man stopped, placing his arms by his side and bowing reverently to mom, towering above her as he softly offered his most profound sympathies. He stood to one side, turning about and directing the bearers up the path and into the house with a sweep of his left arm. I watched intently as the bearers struggled awkwardly to get the coffin through the narrow doorway with some sort of dignity, then listened silently to the clunking and bumping as they manoeuvred the coffin into its allotted position, resting on two dining chairs in front of the window.

The curtains were drawn, and had remained that way since dad had died, only four short days ago. My grandfather stood silently with his brother and the priest. I had noticed him stiffen, wincing as the coffin had banged noisily against the door and the wall of our small living room, just as if he could feel every bump himself. His eyes were red too. Neither he nor his brother acknowledged or spoke to my mom. I thought that strange!

It seemed like an eternity as we shivered in the cold wind, waiting for something to happen. Eventually, one of my uncles appeared at the open doorway and nodded knowingly to the priest. He stepped forward with his black leather bound Psalter held firmly to his chest. My grandfather and his brother took up a position directly behind him as mom ushered Mike and me forward. We followed the priest into the house, walking slowly with our heads bowed, and mom bringing up the rear as he chanted a prayer in nasal Latin.

As I entered the room I froze. The coffin lid was leaning against the kitchen wall, the highly polished brass nameplate shining like a beacon in the half light. I quickly focused my eyes on a plaque hanging on the back wall, not daring to look in the direction of the polished pine coffin. My stomach churned as I made my way to the table, biting hard and gripping Mikes hand so tightly that I could feel my own pulse. The room was very dim, lit only by a single bulb, covered by the speckled glass bowl hanging from the ceiling on three short chains. My mom began to sob uncontrollably as the priest continued his prayers. I turned to face the open coffin, my view obscured by my uncles, their heads bowed and their hands clasped firmly together in silent prayer.

The last time I had seen my dad was Christmas morning, 1958. I did not know at the time that he was terminally ill with Leukaemia. The hospital had let him home for a few hours to be with us. This giant of a man that I had loved so dearly had been reduced to a stooping shuffling shadow of his former self. The mop of thick blonde hair had been replaced by a few thin wisps of silvery grey, exposing most of his scalp. The vitality and permanent smile on his face was no longer there, just a pitiful look of hopeless despair, his cheeks hollowed and his sad eyes gaunt and bloodshot. The usual rosiness of his complexion had gone, giving way to a pale grey, almost off white skin tone that appeared to age him considerably. There was no evidence of the huge chest, the muscular arms and the great strength that had once made him the envy of many of his peers. He had seemed drained as he rested his arms wearily on the back of the settee; struggling for breath as he mumbled slowly. I was shocked at the transformation. This couldn't be my dad!

When the prayers had finished, mom made tea. My granddad led me to the open coffin. My heart pounded in my chest and my stomach churned, a wave of nausea almost overwhelming me as he lifted me to look inside. The priest removed the white diamond shaped lace veil that covered dads face. He looked peaceful, his eyes closed and a contented smile, just as if he had dozed off. He was dressed in an Ivory shroud with gold tassels and a golden belt, his hands crossed on his chest, holding a rosary and a small white bible with a golden cross emblazoned upon it. He looked like a saint. The priest motioned for me to touch dad's hand, but I could not bring myself to it. "He won't hurt you David!" The priest said softly. "That's your dad!" I remained tight lipped and stiff, shaking my head as granddad lifted me nearer the body. I began to struggle, kicking out and shaking my body violently in an attempt to break free of my granddads powerful grip.

The sympathetic caring expression on the priests face changed to one of red faced anger. "Pull yourself together boy" he rasped under his breath as he moved quickly toward me. Everyone was looking at me now. I could see that my granddad was embarrassed, almost ashamed of me. "No. no, please!" I shouted out. "Mom! Mom!" She rushed across to rescue me, giving my granddad and the priest a contemptuous scathing look as she pulled me away, hissing at them. "He's only a bloody boy! He'll say goodbye to his dad when he's good and ready!"

She threw her arms around me, lifted me up and tearfully put me down next to my brother. She rounded on the family, holding Mike and me protectively in front of her as they watched, leaning against the walls and surrounding us like vultures. "Get out, all of you. Just get out and leave us in peace!" Her words echoed around the room. The shocked mourners looked on in silent anger, staring at the three of us as if we had no right to be in such exalted company.

The priest was first to leave, turning as he opened the door, his angry blazing eyes looking straight at my mother. "How dare you! This is no time for family differences Mrs Farrell!" His strong Irish accent sounded harsh, very different to the soothing tones he had initially directed at me. "I will see you tomorrow at your husband's funeral; and may God rest his soul!" My grandfather followed, his face like thunder, muttering inaudibly under his breath as he motioned to his sons to join him, still looking at my mother as if she had no right to be there.

Mom placed the lid carefully back on the coffin. She took the two brass candlesticks off the fireplace, lighting the thick white candles as she placed one at each end of the coffin. She knelt in silent prayer, weeping gently as Mike and I looked on. When she had finished we settled down for the evening, huddling together under a blanket on the settee, keeping the vigil that was customary in my dad's family. I never did understand why we did that; after all, it wasn't as if he was going anywhere!

Mike and I looked very smart in our brand spanking new petrel blue coloured duffle coats with a zip up the front. Mom had got a provident cheque and bought them especially for the funeral. Black gabardine shorts, long grey woollen socks, black Birmingham mail boots, highly polished of course and a black armband to set them off just nicely. We stood once more at the top of the entry, holding hands and watching the mourners arrive, each one contributing to the mound of floral tributes that almost covered our small garden. Although we didn't know half of them we did pretty well out of it, allowing them to pat us sympathetically on the head with one hand and thrust a few coppers our way with the other. Our pockets were positively bulging by the time the tall man in the ribboned top hat appeared at the gate, making his way through the gathering mourners and into the house.

We were called in for one last look at dad before the coffin lid was screwed down for the last time. Once more, I refused the offer to touch him or kiss him on the forehead. I never thought it quite right that people should be milling around the open coffin, chatting nonchalantly and smiling knowingly as they sipped their tea from the cups that we had borrowed from our neighbours. It was almost as if everyone was waiting for him to wake up. Mom had told me that I didn't have to look if I didn't want to, but since I had already been informed that I was the man of the house now I felt it my duty.

This was not the picture of my dad that would remind me of him for the rest of my days. I preferred the happier images of him rattling his tin of corn to feed the pigeons, shouting wildly and waving his arms at the dog races, or just sitting around in the house as Mike and I fiddled with a clockwork train set, marvelling at the improvisation as he put one of moms burning cigarette ends in the chimney of the engine to make it smoke.

I was shivering, half frozen by the icy wind that swept across the cemetery as I stood at the muddy graveside holding my grandfathers hand. The priest continued to drone on in Latin as the coffin was lowered with purple belts into the freshly dug hole by four attendants. All of the women seemed to be crying, especially mom, while the men kept a good old fashioned stiff upper lip. I felt nothing. That wasn't my dad in there, at least, not the dad that I remembered.

One by one the mourners took a small amount of soil from an ornate wooden box, throwing it gently onto the coffin lid as they filed past, speaking their last fond farewells out loud as the priest continued to spout mouthfuls of Latin that nobody understood. Mom cast a white rose as she said her tearful goodbye. As we walked back to the black funeral cars I noticed two men with shovels, smoking as they hid behind a tree, waiting to fill the grave. It all suddenly seemed so matter of fact.

The drive back home was much quicker than the journey here. No detour past the factory where my dad had worked. No crowds of workmates lining the pavement. No slow procession past the place that he had been born, and no church service. Just straight home! After an hour of drinking tea and eating the sandwiches that some neighbours had prepared, people began to make their excuses, re-iterate their condolences and leave. My grandfather was last to leave, placing his hand on my shoulder as he leaned over and whispered to me, reminding me once more that I was the man of the house now. He said nothing to my mother. We were on our own again!

TWENTY THREE
Little scrubber

Mr Starbuck repeatedly banged his fist hard on the wooden locker, shouting noisily as he woke up the dorm in his customary way. I could see that that he was fired up, so I leapt out of bed as he made a beeline straight for me. "Ah, Mr Farrell" he shouted loudly and menacingly, looking down on me, his coal black eyes boring into mine. He poked me in the chest with his hard bony finger as he spoke. "I've got you for a whole weekend!" It sounded like a threat. "We don't like runaways here!" I struggled to keep my feet as his pokes got harder, becoming more painful as he continued to poke the same spot on my sternum. "I want to see you dressed and in the middle of the yard in five minutes with your scrubbing kit and a bucket of cold water. Is that clear?"

I made my first mistake with him by answering back. "But the headmaster said after lunch sir!" I didn't even see his right arm as it swung through the air like greased lightening, slapping me clean off my feet with a single blow, over the bed and onto the floor. "And I said five minutes! Do you understand me boy?" I staggered to my feet breathlessly, covering my sore ear, the tears welling in my eyes. "Yes sir! Five minutes sir!" "Then get on with it" he bellowed, shaking his fist angrily at me as his eyes skirted the dorm for Benny.

Saturday morning. The hands of the large Victorian clock set into the turret of the front tower showed twenty minutes to eight. Benny and I stood on the drainage inspection cover in the middle of the playground, each of us armed with a scrubbing brush, rubber kneeling pad, a large red bar of carbolic soap, a rinsing cloth and a bucket of cold water. We waited, whispering slyly to each other through the sides of our mouths. "He's fackin' well got it in for you mate. You'll have to watch that bastard. He's the worst one of the fackin' lot!" I had already worked that pearl of wisdom out for myself.

Starbuck burst through the washroom corridor door and out onto the playground, his great long strides carrying him quickly toward us as he shouted out his orders, marching erectly and swinging his arms like the ex guardsman that he was. "Farrell! Top left hand corner! Hayes! Top right! At the double you little snots! At the blasted double!" We ran to our respective corners, careful not to spill any of the water for fear of incurring even more of his infamous wrath. "On your knees you little snots, and get scrubbing!"

I was down onto my bright yellow rubber kneeling pad in a flash, wetting the brush, charging it with soap, and sprinkling water onto the hard smooth asphalt in one movement. I began to scrub vigorously, bracing myself as I listened to his approaching foot-

222

steps. "Scrub harder you little snot. Harder!" His well aimed boot caught me square on my freshly caned sore backside, knocking me forward onto the wet playground, causing me to scrape my knees and elbows. I just managed to avoid knocking the bucket over. "I'll make you wish you had never been born before this day is out, you little snot!" I was trembling inside with fear as I quickly crawled back onto the pad and continued to scrub, bracing myself again in anticipation of another boot. I was thankful when he left me to vent his anger on Benny.

Starbuck stood erect under the cover of the verandah, his arms folded tightly across his chest, keeping his beady eyes on our every movement as we continued to scrub our way down opposite sides of the playground. The playground was beginning to fill now as the boys wandered around, their personal ablutions completed, and waiting for the breakfast bell to ring out. When it finally did, I looked up at the evil bastard for some sort of indication that we could go to breakfast. None came, just his icy cold piercing stare and his evil sadistic grin which was obviously his own personal sign language for 'carry on chaps!'

A full ten minutes passed before he re-appeared at the bottom of the playground, bellowing as he ordered us to him at the double. We ran down to him. "I didn't tell you to leave your scrubbing kits up there you little snots!" He screamed as he aimed a slap at me but I managed to parry by moving my head, taking the sting out of the swipe. I quickly turned and ran back up the playground for my scrubbing kit.

Benny did likewise, picking it up and returning to the grinning master as he took great delight in our clumsy attempts to run with it all. He ushered us into the dining hall, making us stand together at the centre pillar, holding our buckets while we waited for the last boy to collect his breakfast.

Collecting your breakfast whilst carrying a full complement of scrubbing kit is not the easiest thing to do, but we managed it as the grinning master and the boys looked on, laughing and tittering as we struggled. I guessed that humiliation was part of his master plan, for I could see from the expression on his face that he was getting a perverse satisfaction out of our predicament.

Eating breakfast without putting your scrubbing kit down is also very difficult, but we managed that too, and even found time for a cup of coffee before once again this devil of a master began bellowing at us. "Times up! Your breakfast's over! Out, out, out! Get moving you little snots! Get back to work!" We scuttled across the dining hall and out through the double doors as quickly as we could for fear of incurring even more of his famous wrath. The sight of the advancing master in the corridor was a more than good enough incentive for us to hurry out into the playground to continue our task!

That day, we scrubbed, and scrubbed, and scrubbed under the watchful eye of Mr Starbuck. When he was not under the verandah or standing right next to us, we knew that he would be watching from some other concealed vantage point, a dormitory or corridor window perhaps, or from the blackness of the locker room maybe, just waiting for one of us to slacken off.

At irregular intervals he would appear from nowhere like a ghost, standing in front of me, mocking and goading, always with the same intimidatory stance, his hands on his hips, legs slightly apart, towering above me as he snarled at me. "Still like running away do you, eh Farrell?" "No sir!" "I can't hear you!" "No sir!" I always shouted louder the second time for I knew that was what he wanted, and I was finding out very quickly that this miserable bad tempered bastard stood for no nonsense whatsoever. Far better to inflate his pathetic ego by appearing pitifully submissive during his crude attempts at brainwashing than it was to risk the end of his boot or a swipe around the chops.

He asked me that same question at least a dozen times during the day. Each time I gave the same answer, the one that I knew he wanted to hear. As the day dragged on I became less fearful of him for I had plenty of time to think as I pressed on with my monotonous task. I thought back to the bullying master at Moseley Road remand home, and how I had gained my revenge on him. I realised that would not happen here for the circumstances were completely different. I could hack anything for three weeks, but three years; that was a different story altogether!

The daily routine continued around us as if we were not there! The boys played football around us after completing their weekend work details and visitors came and went, barely casting a curious eye in our direction, for they had probably seen it all before. We broke only for meals, same routine with the scrubbing kit and the same struggle at the hotplate, the only difference being that we were allowed to wash before eating. By the end of the day we had twice scrubbed the playground from top to bottom.

I was thankful to crawl into my bed that night. It had been a long day. My arms ached, my back ached and my knees were sore. As I lay on my back waiting for lights out, Starbuck grinned his evil grin and wished me a sarcastic, almost menacing good night, and at the same time reminded me that he would see me first thing in the morning. I craned my neck looking for Benny, but he was gone. Spark out!

A heavy dreamless sleep overtook me that night. It seemed that no sooner had I closed my eyes he was there again, banging on the locker, bellowing out his orders and heading straight for me. I leapt out of bed just in time to dodge his swinging right arm. "Stand still you little snot!" I braced my still stiff and aching body as he launched into a verbal tirade, leaning over and pushing his intimidating face into mine. I held firm as he bellowed straight into my face, his strong breath and spittle forcing me to grimace as he continuously poked me again and again in the chest. This time I was determined not to show my fear or pain. "Five minutes, do hear me? Five minutes you little snot!" Another day of scrubbing was about to begin.

I am absolutely certain that ours must have been

the cleanest playground in the whole wide world. Not a square inch of the damn thing lay untouched by our scrubbing brushes at least four times, yet still, it just didn't look any different! I had long since shaken off the feeling of humiliation. I didn't even feel miserable about it anymore. I just got on with it, taking comfort in the fact that this could not last forever, smiling inwardly as I went about my task in the knowledge that the normal routine would restart on Monday morning.

I felt envious when the rest of the boys left for church in the brilliant May sunshine. I had hoped that the powers that be might see more gain in sending us to church, rather than leaving us to repent at leisure on the wrong end of a scrubbing brush. As they were marched off, the Catholics boarded the mini-bus and sped off for Holy Communion at a different place of worship, so apart from the marauding Starbuck, we were on our own now.

It was quite eerie listening to the sounds of two boys scrubbing away in a large deserted and enclosed playground. The swish of the brushes and the clanking and scraping of the buckets on asphalt as we moved backwards down the incline echoed loudly between the buildings. Every now and again we would hear the sharp steps of the tormenting master clip clopping along a corridor or marching around the perimeter as he returned to check on our progress, shattering the ghostly silence by bellowing loudly as he came into view.

I was even more envious when the boys paraded

for afternoon activities while we scrubbed on relentlessly, monotonously, rising from our knees only to change the filthy water. Starbuck never seemed to tire of mocking, humiliating or intimidating us, but even that was wearing thin now. I just didn't care anymore! Fuck him! I won't always be eleven years old and four foot nothing; but, as they say – That is another story!

ISBN 141208496-2

9 781412 084963